The Teenager's Bookshelf

How to Put Joy Back into Reading

Sue Krumbein

DALE SEYMOUR PUBLICATIONS

Cover design by Deborah Hopping.
Student art adapted by Rachel Gage.

Printed in the United States of America. Published simultaneously in Canada.

ISBN 0-86651-272-1
Order number DS03501

DALE
SEYMOUR
PUBLICATIONS
P.O. BOX 10888
PALO ALTO, CA 94303

abcdefghi-MA-89321098765

Contents

Introduction

Question: Is it too unrealistic and idealistic to expect that all of my seventh and eighth grade English students will read more this year than they ever have before—and love it? Yes, most of my colleagues would say. Unless kids already love books, reading is not an activity that the teacher can do much to foster, especially by the upper elementary or high school years. Love of reading is an academic value that is developed early.

Uncomfortable with this generally pessimistic attitude prevailing among my fellow teachers, I set out to prove them wrong. I couldn't accept the notion that some people just don't like to read. I wanted to encourage my students to read. I wanted them to love reading. I felt that if the students in my classes read books they enjoyed, they would want to read *more* books they would enjoy. A cycle would begin, and no one would have to convince them to read—they would be doing it because they wanted to.

Over the years, I have had a number of students who loved to read and who eagerly shared with me their reaction to a particular book. Our discussion of the book was one that interested both of us, one we both enjoyed. This was the type of experience I wanted all my students to have. I wanted them to read *and* to share their reading with me, with their classmates, with their friends, with their parents. It isn't enough to read a book; talking about it with someone else, especially someone who has read it, gives infinitely greater pleasure. Of course, when this happens, the other person generally has a recent reading experience to share as well, so that both parties benefit from the conversation.

This sharing of books with one another is an essential part of my whole approach to teenagers and reading. There's a corollary, too: I know I cannot successfully share books with a class unless I am reading the books they enjoy. That has meant a shift in my reading habits. Some years ago, I began reading the books that I saw my students reading. I'd take two or three books home over the weekend, and I'd have no trouble finishing them because, fortunately, most of the books could be read quickly. They were around 200 pages long and used relatively large print; furthermore, they were *good*. I enjoyed them! I still do. After a while, I knew several popular authors, and I had built up a repertoire of books that I could share with a class. I didn't stop there, though; I continue to read young people's literature, regularly checking the library shelf and my local bookstore for new titles.

It has become a primary goal for me to feel, when June arrives, that most of my students are not only enjoying what they read, but are reading more than ever before. To achieve this end, I have developed a number of techniques and materials that have been extremely successful in stimulating student reading. It is these methods that I want to share in this book.

CHAPTER ONE

Getting Started

Of course, the hardest part of doing anything new is getting started—deciding where you should begin. The first logical step is to examine your own, already existing program. What do you currently do about outside reading instruction? Do you assign book reports? Do you require a certain amount of outside reading? What kinds of materials and assignments do you already use? In short, what do you actually intend to do, or if you want to be educational about it, "what are your *objectives*" for your outside reading program?

To evaluate your program and to determine what is available to your students, you need to look at and question several areas.

1. What is your current approach to book reports, if, in fact, you assign them?

2. What type of guidance do you offer your students in selecting books for outside reading?

3. What kind of guidance is offered by the school librarian?

4. What opportunities do you give students to share their thoughts on the books they have read, other than those discussed in class by everyone?

5. Do you make any effort to display different kinds of materials in the classroom, to give your students an idea of good books that others have read?

6. Do you have books available in your classroom that students can check out?

A brief overview of my program will offer you some points of comparison as you consider your own.

I expect each of my students to read twelve books a year, or three books each quarter. That means one book every three weeks. To assure that they explore several different types of reading, I assign different categories each quarter. Categories I have used include general fiction, nonfiction, survival fiction, World War II fiction, and three books by the same living author.

Students are asked to do a book report in an assigned form for each of the twelve books. As I explain in chapter 2, these book reports take a variety of delightful forms—written, spoken, and visual—and are projects that students genuinely enjoy.

Additionally, I ask each student for a *book talk* once during the school year. A book talk is an oral presentation with a correlated bulletin board display that focuses on one book or one author, or sometimes on one type of book, such as mysteries. Book talks are intended both to inform the class and to arouse their interest in reading.

Besides doing book reports and book talks, my students periodically fill out book recommendation cards on titles they have read and enjoyed. These cards serve as guides for other students looking for new things to read. They are part of the bulletin board display we maintain in the library with the librarian's full cooperation.

This library bulletin board offers a place to display students' art and written book reports, as well as a place to file book recommendation cards. These work together to create an interest in what can be found on the library shelves. We change the display every three weeks when new book reports are collected and new recommendation cards are filled out. The bulletin board not only assists *my* students in finding books, it also serves our entire student body.

To give students some idea of books and authors they might consider reading, I give my own in-class book talks. I might put up articles and pictures about mysteries or maybe a display on Paul Gallico, a favorite author. In my remarks, I'll talk about books I especially like, and I'll give students a bit of information about them. I might even have at hand a book I'm willing to lend, or a list of what is available in the library. I will also present a book talk in the library at the beginning of any period during which we will select books. I choose a wide variety of books so that I will be addressing the needs of all students, regardless of their reading level.

With the help of colleagues, I periodically put together special dramatic presentations, consisting of mock interviews with a character in a novel. This has proven to be a powerful form of presentation, and never fails to interest at least some students in reading the book we have introduced. Later, students present their own oral book reports in this same fashion.

Although our library has a good collection of suitable fiction and nonfiction, I have found it helpful to have my own classroom library as well, so I keep a paperback shelf from which students may borrow books. These books are heavily read each year.

That's the overview of my program. It includes the following essential features:

—book reports in several different forms
—teacher book talks
—student book talks
—a classroom bulletin board for book talk displays
—a library bulletin board
—book recommendation cards, prepared by students
—dramatic presentations involving characters from selected novels
—a classroom paperback collection

Now think about your own program. What features does it include? Are there elements you would like to add, delete, or alter? Often, adding something to your present program is the easiest and most effective way to improve it. One simple way to begin would be to get help from your librarian in developing an outside reading list or in creating a bulletin board in the library that would assist students in choosing books. Maybe you prefer to change something in your program; for example:

1. You might modify the book report assignments that you presently use.
2. You might assign more oral book reports to increase the amount of sharing that goes on.
3. You might assign weekly book talks.

This book offers ideas from my experience that can help you add to or change your outside reading program. Every one of these ideas has worked in my classroom to increase the interest in reading among my students. I believe my approach can do the same for you.

Before we begin exploring in detail the separate features of my program, let me insert a word about prerequisite skills. In order to be successful in the projects I describe, students must be involved in an ongoing program of instruction in the three basics of written, spoken, and visual communication:

1. How to write a well-organized essay or composition of one to five paragraphs.

2. How to organize an outline for an oral presentation, including an introduction, supporting details, and a conclusion.

3. How to design and complete simple art projects using both drawings and lettering.

Clearly, assignments completed for the books students read at the beginning of the year won't be as good as those they do later on; however, I still want their first work to be *good*, something they can take pride in. Even when there is more to be learned and improvements to be made, students should be able to complete book reports, book talks, and art projects at a competent level. This will only happen if you take pains to provide instruction in the areas listed above.

CHAPTER TWO

Book Reports

GUIDING STUDENTS' BOOK SELECTION

One of the purposes of my outside reading program is to get students to explore a variety of books and authors they might not otherwise try. Left to their own devices, some students will choose to read a narrow selection of books, for example only science fiction, or mystery, or adventure. Others will choose books at too easy a reading level. To avoid such problems in book selection, I assign specific types of books to be read at different times of the year. Assigned a certain category of reading each quarter, the students still have choices, but within more limited areas. Thus, the students are encouraged to read more widely than they might choose to do on their own.

During the first quarter, I ask all students to read fiction. This gives me an opportunity to discover their reading taste, if they have developed one, and to observe the difficulty level of the books they choose. For the other quarters, my goal is to assign categories for book reports that will correlate well with my plan for in-class reading assignments, as well as to give students a wide variety of reading experiences. This can be done for students at any grade level. For my seventh graders, the requirements are usually as follows:

1st quarter   any fiction
2nd quarter   survival books, fiction or nonfiction
3rd quarter   general nonfiction
4th quarter   books of their choice

Eighth graders read in the following categories:

1st quarter   any fiction
2nd quarter   any nonfiction
3rd quarter   World War II fiction
4th quarter   three books by the same living author

During the quarter that I require my eighth graders to read World War II fiction, they are reading nonfiction books about World War II for their in-class reading assignment. One group reads *The Diary of Anne Frank*, another reads *Farewell to Manzanar*, and the third reads *The Upstairs Room*. Once the quarter is over, every student in the class has read at least four books dealing with World War II and has completed book reports on the three chosen for outside reading. With the amount of class discussion and sharing on the subject, I find that all the students finish the quarter with a far greater knowledge and understanding of that period of history. The tie-in with social studies is obvious. This system would work equally well with any period in history that you choose to have them study.

I have a similar cohesive unit of study for my seventh graders. During the quarter that they are required to read survival fiction or nonfiction for their book reports, they are reading a survival fiction novel for their in-class reading assignment. By the end of the quarter, each student has explored four different circumstances involving survival and has seen how different people deal with survival situations. They have a far greater understanding of the topic after doing this reading, especially since they have the chance to share their own ideas in class discussion and through their written, visual, and oral book reports.

Assigning general categories is one guide to book selection; I also offer students more specific help in finding something they like in the library. Since the assigned three book reports per quarter require the reading of one book each three weeks, we spend class time going to the library at three-week intervals to choose books. At the beginning of each visit I spend approximately ten to fifteen minutes giving a book talk to acquaint them with a number of authors to consider. I find that this talk assists many students in finding books. I always include authors who write at varying degrees of difficulty so that all students will have some choice among the books I have presented. Also, at the beginning of the year or the start of each quarter, I hand out a list of authors to be considered.

In the appendix, I've included sample lists of recommended authors and the books they've written. These are *not* lists for you to hand out to your students; rather, they are to help you get started compiling your own lists. My lists will be of little use to your students if *you* haven't read any of the titles on them. As you peruse my lists, I am sure you will recognize many familiar names; however, those with whom you are not familiar are also worth a look. They represent a variety of styles, subject matter, and levels of difficulty. Students read at many different levels, and a teacher must be prepared to suggest books to the advanced reader as well as to the more reluctant reader. Some of the listed authors write books at a single reading level, but that is not always the case. For instance, Zilpha Snyder wrote many books that were suitable for students from fourth through eighth grade. Then she wrote a series that begins with the book *Below the Root*, which is quite advanced and a challenge for very good readers in the eighth grade. That particular series would be appropriate for a high school student, especially one who likes fantasy and science fiction mixed.

I want to emphasize the need for the teacher to be familiar with many authors and many different levels of books. It is critically important that I be prepared to enjoy books and conversations about them with *all* my students, not just the ones who love to read. Those who love it are not the problem; they would read vast amounts without any requirement at all. It is the more reluctant readers who benefit most from our sharing of the reading experience.

While I do spend class time helping students select books from the library, I do *not* allow class time for the actual reading of the books for the assigned book reports. I feel strongly that students should develop good reading habits at home, and I address the subject on Curriculum Day or Back-to-School Night when parents come to school to hear about my program.

You can take a variety of approaches to develop good reading habits in students who are not going to read on their own without assistance. One idea is asking students to keep a reading record in a notebook; the student records the date and time spent reading, and the parent signs it for confirmation. If you use this method, you must check the record on a regular basis to assure that reading is being done. You might also offer a reward to those who read regularly and who increase the amount they read on their own. Such an incentive generally works best when the entire class is involved in reaching the goal and in receiving the reward. I have found that group activities, such as a picnic, a bike ride for ice cream, a softball game, a popcorn party, or half an hour of listening to rock music in class all work well as incentives. I always avoid offering free time or some vague event as a reward. The reward should be one that the class values, something special, something they don't do all the time as a regular activity. It is wise to let the class choose their own reward from several options. You can maintain control by offering only options with which you can live; at the same time, the students will have chosen the incentive that they prefer. I do feel, though, that you should resort to special incentives only if they are absolutely necessary. It is far better when the students push themselves to read without a bribe.

ASSIGNING THE BOOK REPORTS

I have observed that many teachers use book reports as a form of test. Such teachers often assign a book report to check up on the student, to see if the required book has, in fact, been read. Students know this, and bring as much enthusiasm to the report as they would to a final exam. Perhaps a better way of looking at the book report is as a regular assignment like all the others in your lesson plan. The only difference is that the student must draw the subject matter for this assignment from a book read outside of class, rather than from an assignment in a book that everyone reads. It is possible to structure a book report assignment in such a way that the student must *use* the story or ideas from the book. The student will quite naturally read the entire book in order to succeed in the assignment, thus eliminating the whole "testing" issue.

The book report in my classroom is handled like all the other assignments I make. The students first prepare a rough draft that I read and return to them; they then correct the rough draft and copy it over before turning it in. However, unlike other assignments, I never have the entire class doing exactly the same thing. For the book report assignments, I divide the class into three groups. Each group is asked to do a different form of book report for a particular assignment: one group does *art* reports, one *written* reports, and the third *oral* reports. This way, we enjoy all the different types of book reports each time, rather than listening to thirty oral book reports one time and seeing nothing but art book reports another. Furthermore, it saves me from having to read an entire class set of written book reports for any one assignment. There's another advantage to having groups: once the first group has presented their oral book reports, the other students have a good idea of what approaches worked well and what they should try to avoid. That is, they have learned from the experience of the first group. This is equally true of the art and the written book reports, since they are displayed on the bulletin board and become models for other students' work.

To give you a clearer picture of how this three-group rotation works, here is a sample chart that might appear on my book report assignment sheet for one quarter.

	FIRST BOOK REPORT	SECOND BOOK REPORT	THIRD BOOK REPORT
ROUGH DUE	Sept. 17	Oct. 8	Oct. 29
FINAL DUE	Sept. 24	Oct. 15	Nov. 5
WRITTEN	Group 1	Group 2	Group 3
ORAL	Group 2	Group 3	Group 1
ART	Group 3	Group 1	Group 2

Within the general categories of written, oral, and art book reports, there are a great variety of projects that students can do. I usually assign a specific type of report in each category to give students some direction. Examples of these are given in the following pages, along with descriptions and illustrations of ways my students have fulfilled the assignments.

ORAL BOOK REPORTS

Oral Report 1
Become the main character and talk to us about your life, your experiences, your friends. Please wear or use something that the character would have worn or used. Prepare an outline.

When Christl read a biography of Benjamin Franklin for an oral book report, she gave a speech that everyone in the class enjoyed. She wore a powdered colonial wig and wire-rim glasses. As she talked about her experiences, we felt almost as if Ben himself were there. The speech was informative, interesting, funny, and very successful.

Oral Report 2
Review your book. Take a point of view and explain how and why you hold that view. Be specific when you give examples. Avoid saying that it was a good or bad book. Your main idea might include a comment on outstanding characters, exciting adventures, funny situations, or anything about which you can give examples. Prepare an outline.

In an oral book report on *Stranger with My Face* by Lois Duncan, Jenny explained to us that the use of astral projection in the novel made it both unusual and exciting. Most young people are very interested in all kinds of ESP, so the mere mention of astral projection got the attention of the class. They were eager to hear an explanation of this phenomenon, about which they knew very little. This became one of the most popular books in our class.

Oral Report 3
Become a character in the novel and talk about how your life has been affected by World War II. Include things that have affected your family as well as your community. Prepare an outline.

Obviously, this assignment relates to my World War II fiction unit. It could be adapted to other units as well.

Judith Kerr has written a series about a family who left Germany to escape Hitler's rule. When Michelle read *The Other Way Round*, the second book in the series, for a book report, she talked about the advantages that moving had for the children in the family: they learned to speak French and then English; they also had the opportunity to live in many different places. On the other hand, moving had many disadvantages for the adults. They lost jobs, homes, and friends, all of which were hard to replace. Michelle was able to contrast the effect of the war on children versus adults. It was an interesting and impressive speech.

Oral Report 4
Prepare an interview using one of the characters in your book as the subject. Write an introduction. Then write questions that an interviewer could ask this character. Try to write questions that would give the character the opportunity to explain situations, problems, activities that were a part of his or her life. Jot down any information that the character might say in answer to each question. Finally, prepare a conclusion. You need to find a classmate to act as the interviewer. You will be the character from your book. You might consider wearing a costume.

Peter and Todd presented an interview based on Charles Crawford's book *Letter Perfect*. Peter played the role of interviewer, and in that role he was a police officer. Todd played B.J., one of the boys in the story. They presented a scenario in which the police officer was questioning B.J. in order to find out about his role in a blackmailing scheme that B.J. and two friends had set up as a prank. The way Peter questioned Todd made it clear that he wanted information; he also conveyed the air of an official who was not pleased with the boys' prank. It was equally clear that Todd, acting as B.J., wavered between cocky and scared, which was exactly the way B.J. felt about the situation. Todd and Peter did a nice job of establishing the atmosphere of the story for the class.

This assignment generally works best if students have already seen you and a colleague perform a similar interview, as I describe in chapter 4.

Oral Report 5
Pretend that you have just moved next door to one of the characters in your book. Tell us how you feel about getting to know this person. What does the person do? What traits have you already observed? Prepare an outline.

When Lisa read *Girl with the Silver Eyes* by Willo Davis Roberts, she gave an oral book report in which she explained her feelings about her new neighbor, a girl with very unusual eyes. She explained that Katie seemed nice, but she certainly looked strange. While Lisa didn't want to be standoffish, she thought she'd see if there were other girls in the neighborhood before she struck up a friendship with Katie. As we listened to Lisa talk about this girl, we got a clear picture of Katie as someone who appeared just like anyone else, *until* you looked into her eyes. We knew that if we'd been in Lisa's position, we too would probably have been put off by a person with silver eyes; however, we also felt sorry for this girl who was oddly different.

Oral Report 6
Talk about several of the books you have read this year, including the one that you have just finished. You might group them by type, or talk about those written by the same author, or describe the ones you especially liked. How do you feel about those particular books? Did they have good characters, interesting situations? Include specific information from each book, rather than general comments. Prepare an outline.

Diane loved to read Lois Duncan books during her year in seventh grade. She gave her final oral book report on the Lois Duncan books she had read, including *Killing Mr. Griffin, Stranger with My Face, Down a Dark Hall*, and *Daughters of Eve*. She began her speech by explaining that although Lois Duncan's books vary, she writes mainly mystery; however, the types of mysteries do differ. Diane then went on to explain the mystery in each of the four Lois Duncan books she had read. She concluded by telling us the additional books by Lois Duncan that she planned to read during the summer when she had lots of free time. Her enthusiasm for this author was obvious—and contagious.

You have seen that for each of the oral book report assignments, I ask students to prepare an outline that they are to hand in for correction before presenting their speech. Here is a sample outline to give you an idea of what I expect. It is the outline Michelle prepared when she did oral book report 3.

I. Introduction
   Anna's family moved several times during World War II. It wasn't that they wanted to move. They had to. They were Jews who were refugees from Hitler's Germany. Anna and her brother Max benefited from the moves, but their parents didn't.
II. Moving
   A. Paris
      1. Language
      2. Housing
      3. School
      4. Jobs
      5. Feelings about France
   B. London
      1. Another new language
      2. British attitude toward refugees
      3. No jobs
   C. Benefits for children
      1. Few set ideas
      2. Learned languages easily
III. Conclusion
   Although Anna's family found their status as refugees very upsetting, Anna and her brother Max benefited from moving to new places. Judith Kerr shows this different reaction of adults and children in her book *The Other Way Round.*

ART BOOK REPORTS

Art Report 1
Create a postcard that has a drawing on one side and information on the other. The drawing should be a scene that you could imagine while reading your book. The writing should be a message from one character to another that is short and to the point

since it has to fit on one side of a postcard. Include the title and author of the book on the side with the writing.

The Arm of the Starfish by Madeleine L'Engle

Dear Adam,
Please help me. I've been wrong about everything. I know my father is doing things that aren't right. He is trying to steal some notes on regeneration from Dr. O'Keefe to sell to another country. Please try to stop him from doing anything wrong.

Kali

For her postcard Alison drew a starfish, which was the creature being used in a research project. The dolphins pictured were friendly and would swim and play with the children who lived on Gaea, where their father was doing this research. Adam Eddington, a 17-year-old boy, came to Gaea for the summer to work on the research project. A girl named Kali used and tricked Adam, and the message on this postcard is one she might have sent him in an effort to get him to behave in a certain way.

Art Report 2
Create a poster showing a hazard to avoid that you learned about in the survival novel you read. Be creative about the way you present your information. Include the title and author of the book in the poster.

Chris read *The Outsiders* by S. E. Hinton for this assignment. He decided that weapons were the hazard to avoid for kids living in the ghetto. He drew a poster showing a "Greaser" being attacked by two "Socs" who were holding weapons—one a knife, the other a broken bottle. In two bubbles, he wrote the threats that the two "Socs" were making to the frightened "Greaser." The poster showed the hazard very clearly.

Art Report 3
Make a drawing depicting a scene from World War II as experienced by the characters in the novel you read. Include a caption if it makes the poster clearer. Also include the title and author of the book on the poster.

After reading *The Other Way Round* by Judith Kerr, Rhonda drew a picture of the London apartment building in which Anna and her refugee family lived. She showed it during a bombing raid, indicating that bombs were a real danger for residents of London during World War II.

Art Report 4
Draw a cartoon with three or more pictures that show an incident or situation from the story. You may use captions or conversation in balloons, comic-strip style. Make sure that the idea is clear. Include the title and author of the book.

For *The Pistachio Prescription* by Paula Danziger, Sandra drew a cartoon showing Cassie and her mother shopping. A boy comes up to them and compliments Cassie's mother on her necklace. This reminds Cassie that her mother is gorgeous and looks very young, which irritates the girl.

Art Report 5
Create a two-layer picture-wheel for the book you read. To do
this, cut two 8-inch (20 cm) circles from tagboard.

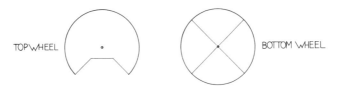

Cut a window in one wheel as shown. This window-wheel will go
on top when you fasten the two wheels together. Draw one picture on the top wheel, showing something important from the
story. Divide the bottom wheel into four equal parts and draw
four more pictures about the story. Each drawing should be
related in some way to your picture on the top wheel. Finally,
fasten the wheels together by poking a metal brad through the
centers. This will allow each wheel to turn.

The point is to create a series of drawings that work together to
tell something about the story. As we turn the wheel, we should
see the relationship between the top picture and each of the
drawings that shows through the window. Be sure to include the
title and author of the book on the top wheel.

For her wheel on *Below the Root*, Gwen drew the Grundtree on
the top wheel. The Grundtree was the main living and working
area of the community of Greensky. It was where everything happened. In her first picture on the bottom wheel, she drew three

characters who lived in Greensky and played a major role in the story. In the second picture, she showed us the root below the main trunk of Greensky, a dangerous place since it was close to the evil Pash-an who lived below the root. The third picture was the Ol-zhaan, the rulers of Greensky, who were keeping important information from their people, especially in regard to the Pash-an. The last picture showed a citizen of Greensky gliding on his shuba, a means of transportation in his community.

Art Report 6
Create a greeting card that could be sent to one of the characters in your book. Include a design or picture as well as a message. It can be any kind of card, not necessarily one for a standard occasion such as a birthday. The card should fit the character and the situation. Include the title and author on the back of the card with your name.

Gaby, having read *The Girl with the Silver Eyes*, designed a card for Katie to send Louise on her birthday. Katie, the girl with the unusual silver eyes, discovers there might be other children with this same quality and tries to find them. She meets Louise who is also unusual, but they don't live close enough to be friends. That's why she sends her a birthday card.

Art Report 7
Make a bookmark out of tagboard. It should have two parts. On the top, draw a design relating to the story. On the bottom, include the title, author, and a statement or two about the book.

Most students cut a piece of tagboard which has a shape on the top related to the story—a cat for *The Cat Ate My Gymsuit*, a dagger for *The Outsiders*, a wolf for *Julie of the Wolves*. The bottom is rectangular to fit in the book.

Art Report 8
Put together a display of pictures, maps, and books on the subject about which you read. You may make a counter display or one to put on the bulletin board. Everything in the display should be clearly labeled. Include the title and author of the book you read.

Stacey read *Eric* by Doris Lund, a biography of a boy with leukemia who struggled mightily to conquer the disease. Her display included a sign with the title and author, an explanation of leukemia, and a medical report on Eric written on an actual hospital form she'd managed to obtain. This was an interesting way to share information about the book with the class.

Art Report 9
Create a rebus. First write some information about the book you
read, perhaps a paragraph. Double-space what you write. Then
replace as many words as possible with puzzle drawings for the
reader to decipher. Be as creative and clever as you can be.
Include the title and author.

Here is a translation of Marya's rebus on *Bridge to Terabithia*:

> The book *Bridge to Terabithia* was a very touching book by Katherine Paterson. Jess was the fastest kid in the fifth grade, until Leslie Burke moved in. She was the first girl to run in the races and beat anybody. Jess and Leslie became good friends and decided to create a kingdom of which they would be rulers. To enter into Terabithia, you had to cross the creek by swinging across on a rope. Their relationship was quite unusual, because of their age. The only time they could be close was in Terabithia.
>
> Katherine Paterson has written about a very uncomfortable situation between girls and boys.

Art Report 10
Create a design related to your book that can be done as shrink art. Draw your design on a piece of paper, making it no larger than 6 × 8 inches (15 cm × 20 cm). Color in the design so that you can trace it onto the plastic sheet. The design you choose should illustrate something about the book that other people might find interesting to look at. Write some information on an index card, explaining the relationship between your art work and your book. When you have finished putting your design on the plastic, check the shrink-art box for heating directions. Punch a hole in the top of the plastic before heating so that you can hang your finished piece on a piece of yarn attached to the index card.

Shrink-art materials can be purchased at a hobby or crafts store or anywhere with a crafts department, such as some toy stores. There are two types of plastic sheets, clear and opaque. The clear requires permanent markers for the application of the design. With the opaque, the student uses colored pencils. I always purchase the materials, paying for them myself or charging them to petty cash if our school budget can afford it. I also supply marking pens or colored pencils for this project, depending on which type of plastic I purchase. The shrinking is done in an oven. It is important to follow the directions, but it is very easy. Sometimes I shrink the design for the student; sometimes the student takes it home to shrink it. Encourage students to make their designs very colorful as these look much better than line drawings when they are shrunk.

The Good Earth

The Good Earth by Pearl S. Buck relates how a simple farmer in China struggled to establish a family which would one day become a powerful dynasty. It is a very real and moving story. Even in the end when Wang Lung is no longer a farmer but a rich and famous man, he knows and understands that his fortune was entirely provided by the good earth.

Gwen Rino

WRITTEN BOOK REPORTS

Written Report 1
Write a character sketch of someone in your book. Identify one particular trait of the person about whom you are writing and then show, through plenty of supporting details, that he or she definitely has that trait. Include such possible information as how the person treats others, what the person does in certain circumstances, how the person reacts to people and events.

When Chrissie read *Dragonwings* by Laurence Yep, she stated in her introductory paragraph that Moon Shadow, a young Chinese boy who had just recently joined his father in San Francisco, faced many challenges in his new world. She went on to explain that Moon Shadow had to learn how to handle comments made about him by the "demons" he encountered. Next, she talked about the difficulty he had in learning English. Her third supporting paragraph explained Moon Shadow's father's desire to fly and the difficult role Moon Shadow played in that dream. Chrissie's essay was clear to any reader, regardless of whether or not the person had read the book.

Written Report 2
**Write five journal entries as if you are one of the characters in
your book. The entries should be sequential. By that I mean you
should follow the order of events as they happened, not jump
around. Please include your feelings about what is happening as
well as details of the events.**

After reading *Cranes in My Corral*, Jeb wrote the following journal as Dayton Hyde, the author of the book. When other students
read it, many of them checked out the book because of how interesting the journal sounded.

April 4. I have four crane eggs that I hope will hatch. The
hens are sitting on them, and they seem perfectly content. It
would be a real accomplishment to raise sandhill cranes.
They're a very endangered species.

April 20. Four cranes hatched today. I named them Eeny,
Meeny, Miney, and Moe. The smallest, Moe, is a bit puny
compared to the others, but they are all healthy and have
taken to feeding rather well. Raising them could be quite a
challenge.

May 20. As I suspected they might, the cranes have inter-
rupted the regular routine at the ranch. They interrupt me,
no matter what I'm doing. They seem to feel that I'm their
mother. They follow me, peck at me, and generally make a
nuisance of themselves. It would seem logical to teach them
to fly soon.

June 2. Today, I gave the cranes their first flying lesson. All
went well until I was flapping my arms and actually raised
myself into the air about three feet. The unfortunate part was
that I fell into a heap, and that immediately caused my
cranes to gather round me, pecking my face and expressing
their concern. I feel a bit sore tonight.

September 25. The cranes have migrated south. Although I
know that's their natural instinct, I'm worried. They trust
humans, which is unwise. They could walk right up to a
hunter, unaware of the danger. I've made a few inquiries, but
so far I haven't talked to anyone who has seen my cranes. I'll
continue to search for them, and I hope to hear good news
soon.

Written Report 3
**Write an essay on the problems faced by one who lived during
World War II. These could be large or small problems. Write**

only about the problems that you learned about in reading your book. Use the five-paragraph essay format.

When Ian read *Mila 18* for one of his World War II fiction books, he wrote an outstanding essay. His main idea was that the Jews in the Warsaw ghetto had many problems on a day-to-day basis. The problems about which he wrote were food, safety, and sanitation. After reading the essay, anyone would have a clear view of what life for Jews in Warsaw was like during World War II.

Written Report 4
Write a review of the book that you read. DO NOT begin with a general comment such as "The book was good." DO decide on a specific comment that you can support with details from the book, such as the fact that the author created some very funny situations, or that the characters had some very exciting adventures. Use the five-paragraph essay format.

In a review of Lois Duncan's *I Know What You Did Last Summer*, Lisa stated that the author writes a very good mystery. The book, she explained, is suspenseful, mysterious, and intriguing. She went on to tell which aspects of the story could be described with each of these three words.

Written Report 5
Write a letter as if you are one of the characters in your book writing to someone you know or to someone about whom you have heard. What you say will depend on your relationship with this person. If you are fairly close, talk about the things you have been doing that would interest the person. If you are less familiar with the person you are writing to, relate some information that you think would interest him or her. Remember to begin the letter with a greeting appropriate to the situation. Please include the title and author of the book after the closing of your letter.

In Jenny's letter based on *Stranger with My Face*, she takes the role of Laura, writing to her friend Helen, who is in the hospital. Helen knows about a very unusual situation in Laura's life, so that's what Laura talks about. Laura's twin sister, whom Laura has never met, is trying to communicate with her through astral projection, a phenomenon in which one person projects her personality out of her body into someone else's. Lia, the twin sister, is clearly an evil individual, but Laura is greatly intrigued by her presence.

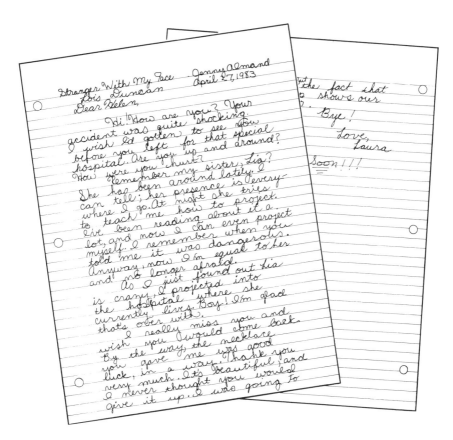

Written Report 6
Write a report on one aspect of the subject you read for this non-fiction assignment. Use the form of a five-paragraph essay, writing a longer essay if necessary. Choose a very specific topic rather than covering the subject generally. For example, suppose you read a book on having a raccoon as a pet. An essay on "the type of pet a raccoon makes" would be too general. If you chose to write about "the problems a raccoon owner might have," that would be suitably specific. Another example of a specific topic on raccoons would be "the traits that make a raccoon a fine pet."

When Carl read *Rascal* by Sterling North, he did write an essay about the problems a person would have with a raccoon as a pet. He included information on stealing, something common to raccoons. He also talked about the complaints of neighbors regarding the raccoon's behavior. Finally, he explained the need for the raccoon to remain a wild animal.

Those are the oral, art, and written book report assignments that I have used in my classroom with happy results. Likely you have similar assignments of your own that can offer students an enjoyable alternative to the standard "This book was about . . ." book report. My decision on which type of report to assign is generally based on what books I have asked the students to read. For example, if the students are reading survival books, it is very appropriate for them to do the journal assignment, taking the point of view of a character in the book, for it is reasonable to believe that a person in a difficult situation might keep just such a record of events. Similarly, when reading World War II fiction, it works out well for a student to give a speech about the problems that were created for a story character's family because of the fighting. As an oral book report, that assignment is very effective.

The book report, done as a creative project, is one important way in which student reading can be guided, encouraged, and increased. However, it is by no means the only way. The remaining chapters describe the other key features of my program for motivating more outside reading, starting with the idea of the book talk.

CHAPTER THREE

Book Talks

Generally speaking, when I give an assignment to a student, my assumption is that the individual will benefit from doing the assignment. This is definitely the case with the book talk, as it is with all the other assignments in my outside reading program. But there's an added bonus with the book talk: everyone else in the class benefits as well. Perhaps that is the most important feature of oral reports. Not only does the speaker learn from organizing and presenting the material, but the rest of the class also hears about a book or an author that someone else especially enjoyed. Often, the speaker's enjoyment is infectious, prompting other students in the class to try the same book.

The role of the book talk in my program is to present one book, one author, or one type of book each week, in order to inform and interest the class in reading some titles they otherwise might not be aware of.

There's a very good reason to encourage plenty of book talks that focus on specific authors rather than on single titles. As you may have observed, many authors of young people's fiction write several books in a series. I believe that they do this in order to write books of manageable length for young readers, but still be able to tell a rather long and perhaps complicated story. Judith Kerr's series about a family of refugees in World War II is but one example. Madeleine L'Engle's popular and award-winning *A Wrinkle in Time* is the first book in a series of three. Susan Cooper has written a wonderful series that begins with *Over Sea Under Stone* and continues through four more books; Zilpha Snyder has a three-book series that begins with *Below the Root*. Bette Greene first wrote *Summer of My German Soldier*, then followed it with a sequel, *Morning Is a Long Time Coming*. Everyone who read those books loved them.

Occasionally, the last book in a series is more of a rehash than it is a continuation of the story. This is always disappointing; however, it is not usually the case.

In their younger years, students may have chosen books by title, by cover, or by length, paying little or no attention to the author. In my classes, I want to reverse this. I actively encourage my students to become familiar with many different authors. What I am aiming for is that they select a book on the basis of recognizing the author. I want them to learn that if they enjoyed one book by a particular author, chances are good that they'll like other books written by the same person. When they begin a series, they generally will read all the books in the series and find the experience very satisfying. Such a mindset is by no means limited to teenagers; in fact, Crystal Thrasher has a series of three books about a family living through the depression, and I have read each book as it was published. I am sure there is to be a fourth book in that series, and I admit that I am very eager to find it on the "new books" shelf one of these days. It is this sort of enthusiasm that I hope to engender in my students. Once they begin to anticipate the joys of reading, they are not likely to stop.

I do the initial book talks myself during the first four weeks of school. This acquaints the students with a variety of approaches and also allows them time to think about what subject they might choose for their own book talks. In the fifth week, I post a list of names and dates for book talks. I also review the assignment so that it is clear to everyone exactly what it entails. Basically, the book talk assignment I give to the students is as follows:

1. Create a poster that will be put up on our special Book Talk Bulletin Board on Monday of the week you're assigned to give a book talk. This poster should depict information on the book or the author who is to be featured in your talk. The poster should be both attractive and informative. (I generally supply construction or ditto paper to the students, if necessary. I suggest that the poster be approximately 9 × 12 inches. They use their own pens or colored pencils to complete the poster.)

2. Prepare a talk that you will give to the class on Tuesday. Be sure to plan and practice what you are going to say. Include specific details about your subject that will interest the rest of us. Use the book talk outline form to organize your material.

3. Bring to class the book or books that you are featuring— either borrowed from our library or your own copies.

Each student has a copy of this assignment during the first four weeks when I am giving demonstration book talks. After my first talk, I ask a few questions to see if they have recognized my introduction and conclusion. I also ask about the overall organization of my talk to see if they have followed the points I was making. I then teach a specific lesson on organizing a book talk. I emphasize these points:

1. Deciding on a main idea.
2. Stating that main idea in an introduction.
3. Organizing points of support for the main idea.
4. Restating the main idea in a conclusion.

The book talk outline form reinforces these four points.

Book talk outline form

Topic:

I. Introduction

II. Support

   A.

   B.

   C.

III. Conclusion

I want to be sure that my students understand the assignment before they have to do it. A book talk should be a successful experience for the speaker and for the rest of the class as well. To achieve that end, I review the points on organization after my second, third, and fourth book talks.

By the fifth week of school, it is time for the students to begin giving their own book talks. Even though the list of names and dates for book talks is posted, I always remind the student whose turn is next an entire week before the assignment is due. I do this by putting the student's name on my weekly assignment board, along with the dates that the poster goes up and the book talk is to be given. Since I always review the assignment board aloud after the students have copied it down onto their assignment sheets, I am sure to remember to mention the following week's book talk to the appropriate student.

If the person next scheduled to do a book talk is a very competent student, I merely supply a copy of the book talk outline form and remind the student where I keep the art supplies that can be used for the poster. I always inquire into the student's plans for the talk, prepared to offer assistance if I sense that it is needed. If the next scheduled speaker is a weak student, I will set up a specific timeline for him or her to follow in preparing the assignment. I give such a student the book talk outline form a full week before the book talk is due, asking that the student fill it out and share it with me on the Tuesday of the week before it is due. If the outline is satisfactory, I commend the work and offer some suggestions about ways to learn the material for the talk. If the outline is *not* acceptable, I ask the student to stay after class long enough for us to make some changes. Remember that, by this point, I have already taught outlining to my class. I have also taught them how to organize the book talk, so what I need to do with the student now is all review. With some prior work in outlining, it is not terribly difficult for most students to do a reasonable job of organizing their material.

Notice I mention in the previous paragraph that I expect students to *learn* their material for the book talk. I require this in order to eliminate any reading of the talks. I want a *speech*, not just a written report read aloud. The only way to get students to give a speech, to look at us and talk to us, is to eliminate the use of notes or an outline. This system has worked beautifully in my class. Done correctly, the book talk is like a conversation the student is having with us.

I am including here a sample book talk outline; it is one I displayed for students to look at when I gave a book talk on Bette Greene.

Topic: Bette Greene

I. Introduction
   Bette Greene has written several books, but I really enjoyed two of them, *Summer of My German Soldier* and *Morning Is a Long Time Coming*. They tell the story of Patty Bergen.

II. Support
   A. Who Patty is
      1. Teenage girl

      2. Lives in Jenkinsville, Arkansas
      3. Very smart
  B. Meeting Anton
      1. German POW
      2. Escapes
      3. Hiding him
      4. Talking about his family
  C. Eventual complications in life
      1. Sent to juvenile detention center
      2. Estranged from family
      3. Continuation of story in *Morning Is a Long Time Coming*
III. Conclusion

Not only is *Summer of My German Soldier* a good book, but Patty Bergen is a very interesting girl. You'll enjoy getting to know her in these two books by Bette Greene.

The sequence for completing a book talk assignment, then, is this:

—*Monday before due date:* Alert next speaker. Hand out book talk outline form. Discuss preliminary plans.

—*Tuesday before due date:* Review outline with student, if necessary (for weaker students only).

—*Entire week before due date:* Student works on poster and on learning the material for the talk.

—*Monday (poster due date):* Student puts up poster before class begins.

—*Tuesday (talk due date):* Student hands in outline (only rough draft is required) and opens class with a book talk.

After each book talk, there is usually a lot of class discussion. Sometimes other students have read books by the same author and want to say something about them. Often, students have questions to ask the speaker. The book talk, combined with the discussion that follows, generally lasts from fifteen to twenty minutes.

To better give you the flavor of this part of my program, let me describe a few of the book talks my students have prepared.

When Peter gave his book talk on Harry Goodrich's book, *A Seal Called Andre*, it was instantly clear to everyone in the class that Peter had very much enjoyed the book. Of course, we already knew that Peter liked animals, but after he told us so many funny things that Andre had done, we realized this would be a good book for any of us to read. The book is a biography in which the author shares the experiences he had with a pet seal. Peter created a very attractive poster, and he displayed a copy of the book. He told us that it was in our school library as well as at the public library. Following Peter's talk on this book, a number of other students read it, too.

Since I require my eighth graders to read World War II fiction for their book reports during one quarter of the year, a number of students always read and enjoy books by Judith Kerr. Michelle read the three-book series that Kerr wrote about a family of refugees and their experiences during World War II. She chose to give her book talk on this series. Her poster focused on the author, and she displayed copies of all three books. On Tuesday, when she talked about the series, Michelle set out to do two things. First she explained the situation of the family featured in these books. Then she shared her feelings about the books individually, concluding that the third book, *A Small Person Far Away*, was the only one she hadn't particularly enjoyed. The other two, *When Hitler Stole Pink Rabbit* and *The Other Way Round*, she thought were very good. While the second book continued the story well, Michelle was disappointed in the way the third book concluded the story. This book talk was very helpful to the class; not only did they learn about some books they might read for their own World War II book reports, they also heard information that might prevent their being disappointed, as Michelle had been, with the final book in the series.

One of the most popular authors among my students is Lois Duncan. She is considered a mystery writer, though her books contain many elements other than mystery. Christie gave her book talk on Lois Duncan. She included on her poster the four Duncan books she had read. Next to the poster, she listed the other Duncan books that she intended to read in the future. By listing the books in different places, she could be sure that students wouldn't ask her about a book she hadn't read. In her talk, Christie told us about the mystery in each of the four books she'd read without revealing "who-dun-it."

This is a critical point: it is very important to teach your students how to review a book *without* summarizing the entire story. No one wants to sit through an elaborate explanation of a plot, all the way through the conclusion. When that happens, the book is spoiled for anyone else who might want to read it. Remind the students that the goal of the book talk is simply to acquaint the class with a particular book, an author, or a certain category of

book, so that in the end everyone will be familiar with many different books, authors, and categories. The ideal result of a book talk is that other students be motivated to read the books that were presented. Help students learn to make their talks tantalizing rather than satiating.

So far, I have told you about successful book talks and attractive posters. As we all know, this is not always what you get. The question is: what do you do when the poster is awful, or even non-existent, and the book talk is poor?

To reduce the chances of getting an impossibly weak display, I set certain minimum standards for the book talk poster. I explain these standards during the first four weeks of school when I am doing all the book talks. To demonstrate, I use my own materials, as well as student posters from past years, as examples. Specifically, I insist that the poster be clearly lettered, including essential titles and author names. It should be colorful so that it catches the eye. The design should be attractive, and it should relate to the topic of the book talk.

The question always comes up about artistic ability. Obviously, some students are much more artistic than others. I do not worry about that; all students can use lettering and color in such a way that their rather simple drawings are perfectly acceptable. (To be honest, when I grade the book talk, the speech always carries more weight than the poster, though I do like to have something attractive on the book talk bulletin board each week.)

When I feel that someone might do an especially poor job on the poster, I review the standards with that student, and I ask about any plans. I find that most of my students will rise to the occasion when I set reasonable expectations. It is better to spend some time with students before they do their posters than to keep them after school making new ones when they prepare a display that you feel is unacceptable. However, in spite of my precautions, every once in a while a very disappointing poster is hung up on Monday. When this happens, I feel no qualms about quietly asking the student to take it down, put it on my desk, and plan to stay after school to redo it or improve it. This won't happen very often if your standards are high and you refuse to accept poor or mediocre work, especially when you know it is the result of carelessness or sheer laziness.

While I am talking about quality, let me also share my feelings about poor speeches. *I do not want to hear them.* For this reason, if a student's speech is absolutely awful, I will ask the speaker to stop, sit down, and see me after class. I will then explain my objections and ask the student to work on the problems, preparing to give the book talk again later in the week. I admit that this rarely happens, but when it does, it is a lesson for all.

As the year goes on, the book talks, like everything else, get better and better. We are exposed to the reading tastes of many different people, and by the end of the year we generally find that our own reading experience is much more wide ranging than it was before. We often will share books, informally, with someone whose reading preferences we have learned about through the book talks. We lend books that we have bought or that we were lucky enough to receive as presents. In short, by year's end, the book talk has opened up many new resources for the willing reader and has stimulated the less enthusiastic student to read more widely. In addition, all students have gained a great deal of speech training. This improves their confidence and self-image as well as their academic skills.

CHAPTER FOUR

Panels and Interviews

While book talks can be easily incorporated into any program to encourage more outside reading, I have developed another form of oral presentation that is so effective, you must give it serious consideration, even though it requires a bit of extra work. I am talking about the dramatic interview or panel discussion, conducted with people who are playing characters from fiction or nonfiction books. Such presentations can be done either by a pair of teachers or by a teacher with selected students.

First, let me explain the dramatic interview. This performance requires only two people; however, both of them must have read the book on which you will base the interview. One person writes the script-outline, which should consist of an introduction of the individual being interviewed, questions for that character, a few notes about possible answers, and a conclusion. Once the basic outline is written, the two people must get together to practice the interview. Generally, the person who writes the outline will do the interviewing, while the other person will take the role of a particular character in the book.

It is important to realize from the start that this interview must be spontaneous on the part of the person taking the role of the character. That person should definitely not need or use notes; the answers to the interviewer's questions will all come from the story, and the person being interviewed ought to be very familiar with those events. You will run through the interview at least once prior to your performance, and in so doing it will become clear to both of you that you really do know a great deal about the character. You will be very likely to fall quickly and naturally into the roles you are playing. That is what makes this style so successful.

At this point you might be wondering why I, much less you, would want to do something like this for a class. The reason is very simple: I have found the interview format to be extraordinarily successful. A colleague and I have presented numerous interviews using a character from a book as the subject, and after each performance, that book has been in great demand by students. Thus, we have accomplished our purpose—stimulating students to read.

The first interview we did was based on the nonfiction book *And I Alone Survived* by Lauren Elder. At that time, the seventh graders were reading survival fiction and nonfiction and the eighth graders were reading general nonfiction, including biography and autobiography. Thus, this book nicely fit both categories. Additionally, both my colleague and I had read and enjoyed the book, so it was an obvious selection for this exercise.

I began by writing up an outline. Then my partner and I got together after school to look over what I'd written and to practice. The interview was scheduled for our library period on Thursday, and we didn't have a great deal of time to prepare. As we ran through the interview, I made notes on the outline in places where I'd improvised and added questions as we went along. Our most important and interesting finding was that, almost immediately, we "became" our characters. I found myself listening intently to "Lauren's" comments and explanations. "She" was telling me about a plane crash in the mountains near Death Valley, in which the pilot of the small plane and his girlfriend were killed. She was able to describe the situation in such a graphic manner that I "believed" every word of it. We both realized the value and impact of the dramatic style we'd adopted and pledged to duplicate it for our classes on Thursday.

Once the students were seated in the library, I began the interview with my introduction of Lauren Elder. I did not speak as the teacher, but as the interviewer, so that we could set the stage immediately. In the first few minutes of our performance, I heard a few titters, but very quickly we had captured our audience. They bought it! By the end of the interview, it was clear that we had totally convinced them that we were Lauren Elder and an interviewer. During the question period, the students directed their questions to "Lauren"—they did *not* use the teacher's name. They asked her questions like these: "Did you ever consider giving up?" "Have you flown in a small plane since this experience?" They spoke to this woman as if she were, in fact, Lauren Elder.

Needless to say, immediately following our presentation there was a run on the book *And I Alone Survived*. We kept it checked out of the public library for weeks, and our school library copy went from student to student. Everyone who read it loved it, just as we knew they would.

This experience gave us the courage to try this type of presentation again. Our second interview involved Patty Bergen, a character in Bette Greene's novel, *Summer of My German Soldier*. This novel is set in the United States during World War II. My eighth graders were reading World War II fiction this quarter, and since seventh graders would also be studying that period when they were in eighth grade, we felt that an interview of Patty Bergen was appropriate for all. The other reason for choosing a character from this novel is that it is an excellent book by a very fine author.

Keep in mind that Patty Bergen is a fictional character. Because of this, the person who plays that part in the interview has the opportunity to develop a style and a personality for the character, based on what traits are revealed in the novel. Perhaps using a fictional character in the interview gives the team a greater range of choice in deciding what to talk about. In the Lauren Elder story, there was little choice. We talked about the plane crash, the single event in her life that led to her writing the book. It was not quite so straightforward in the case of Patty Bergen. Many things happened to her in the novel, even though there was a central, important incident. For that reason, we approached the second interview quite differently from the first. To set the stage, we began with the town in which she lived. I asked "Patty" to tell me about Jenkinsville and what it was like during the summer. I then proceeded to ask her about the POW camp that was built outside her town. From there, I could ask about her meeting the German soldier, Anton.

This second interview was just as successful as the first, perhaps even more so, because many students tend to enjoy fiction more than nonfiction. Also, Bette Greene wrote a sequel to *Summer of My German Soldier* called *Morning Is a Long Time Coming*, in which she does a fine job of continuing Patty Bergen's story. Those who had read both books immediately commented on the fact that the second book was as good as the first, thus giving interested readers even more reason to read the first of the series.

Having been so successful with the interview format, my colleague and I decided to try a panel discussion. We wanted to include students, though we also wanted to be involved ourselves. After talking about several possibilities, we decided on a panel consisting of people who had lived through, who had been affected by, or who had particular opinions about World War II. We set up this panel at the end of the third quarter, when the eighth graders had finished their World War II unit. I again wrote an outline. Once the two of us got together to look at what we had, we felt that a panel with five members plus the moderator would work well. On the panel would be Mr. Frank, Anne's father in *Anne Frank, Diary of a Young Girl*; Jeanne Wakatsuki, the main character in *Farewell to Manzanar*; and Joanna Reiss, the main character in *The Upstairs Room*. We also included an American who felt that the government had done the right thing in shipping the Japanese to internment camps, and we completed the panel with a German soldier.

Perhaps this last panel member was a macabre attempt at humor; however, the humor proved to be a good thing. Our German soldier provided plenty of it without taking away from the serious content of the discussion. He was the only member of the panel who spoke with an accent, and he did it very effectively. This, of course, was funny, and the audience laughed. They also laughed when he spoke very animatedly about the failure of the German army to win the war and about his great feeling of disappointment. The humor stemmed mainly from the use of the accent, but much credit is due the student playing the role—a fine speaker and actor whose dramatic speech and movements could make the most of a situation. In this case, he contributed an often-ignored point of view as well as a lighter atmosphere.

In order to prepare for this panel, we got together with the students to practice answering questions as well as following our format. We especially stressed their doing some acting so as not to appear wooden. We encouraged them to respond vehemently, to sound upset or excited or angry, whatever emotion would seem appropriate. We even suggested that they interrupt one another on occasion to add to the authenticity of the presentation.

As the moderator, it was my job to ask these people questions that would get at their experiences, their feelings, their memories, and perhaps even their plans for the future. I began by asking each person to explain where he or she was during the war. I could then build from that opening bit of information to ask about conditions in an internment camp, about the problems involved in hiding so many people in the center of Amsterdam, about particular feelings of fear while in hiding, about American attitudes towards Japanese-Americans during the war, and about problems the German military had. After a very short period of time, panel members were listening to each other and were eager to react to what someone else had said. As you know, students so often react only to what the teacher says. This method really enabled us to set up a situation where students reaped the benefits of interacting with each other.

The big difference between the interviews we had done and this panel discussion was that students were much more involved in the latter. Since the students did such a good job, we decided to have eighth graders try interviews as their oral book report assignment for the fourth quarter. They basically prepared the same way my colleague and I had done. I have listed this assignment in chapter 3 as one of the options for oral book reports.

In assigning the interview for an oral book report, I was aware that students might not always be able to find, for their interviewer, another student who had read the book. After some thought, I decided this would not be a real problem as long as I allowed some class time for students to practice with the written outline. Students who are attempting this interview assignment must feel comfortable with their partners. If it immediately becomes apparent that the person who has agreed to be the interviewer cannot handle the job, I permit the student to find someone else—with my help, if necessary. I would probably not try this form of oral book report before the fourth quarter. By that time, everyone in the class has heard speeches given by the other students on numerous occasions, giving them ample opportunity to decide with what partner they would be most comfortable. Obviously, many students ask their friends for this type of assistance, and that generally works out fine.

The written work that I require for this assignment consists of an introduction to the character, questions for the interviewer to ask, a few notes indicating what information the character would include in the answer, and a conclusion. Students will likely need some help with all of these, so let's look at each one separately.

THE INTRODUCTION

Ideally, the introduction should both present the person being interviewed and say a bit about him that would justify his being interesting enough to be the subject of an interview. I encourage my students to write down information about the character's experiences, rather than to begin by merely announcing who the person is. As an example, here are the introductions I used in the interviews of Lauren Elder and Patty Bergen:

> Several years ago, Lauren Elder had an experience that was quite amazing. It certainly didn't turn out as she'd planned. The event began in the San Francisco Bay Area on April 26, 1976.

After this introduction, my first question was: "Lauren, I am curious about the reason you were making a flight in a small plane. Where were you going and why?"

Here is the introduction I used in the Patty Bergen interview:

> When people think about World War II and its effect on the civilian population, they usually think of people who lived in Europe where the fighting was taking place. However, right here in the United States, POW camps were built to hold German prisoners. Our guest today, Patty Bergen, lived in a small town in Arkansas in the 1940s, and a POW camp was built right outside her town. It affected her life more than anyone would have thought it could.

After this introduction, my first question was: "Patty, it is good to have you here. Could you begin by telling us what was happening in Jenkinsville during the summer the German POW's arrived?"

THE QUESTIONS

After setting up an introduction, the next step is writing questions. Naturally, I do not want my students to write questions that have single-word answers. I want them to realize that their questions basically have to introduce topics about which the character can talk. That means that the student can write one or two questions on a topic, then go on to something else, using a transition at the beginning of the question that changes the topic. Here are the questions I asked in the Lauren Elder interview. Note the way they move from one topic to another.

1. Lauren, I'm curious about the reason you were making a flight in a small plane. Where were you going and why?

2. What did you wear on the trip?

3. Though I don't believe you knew the pilot very well, can you tell us a bit about him? Jay was his name, wasn't it?

4. I know your plane crashed. What was the actual crash like?

5. What was the condition of the pilot and the other passenger, Jean, after the crash?

6. What did you do the first day, after the crash?

7. On the second day, I know you set off to walk to civilization. How did you feel about your chances of surviving?

8. I was interested to read in your book that you saw many visions as you hiked down the mountain. What were they, and how did you feel about them?

9. I am impressed by your ability to survive such an ordeal. Looking back, how do you feel about it?

Sometimes, a question needs a comment to precede it; other times that is not necessary. You will need to provide some instruction and practice in order for your students to understand how to write questions that suit the interview style.

THE CONCLUSION

In the conclusion of an interview, the interviewer generally expresses pleasure at having had the chance to talk with the individual. This is also an excellent opportunity for the interviewer to tell the audience the title and author of the book in which the person's story is told. For example, here is the conclusion from the Lauren Elder interview:

> It has been very interesting talking to you about your experience, Lauren. I am delighted that you were able to join us. Those of you in the audience who are interested in Lauren's story can read about it in the book she has written called *And I Alone Survived*. It is available in our library as well as at the public library.

Obviously, I am enthusiastic about the panel discussion and interview style as a way of introducing students to a variety of books. Not only does this approach give the entire class an exciting, first-person feel for a book they might read, it also gives the speakers an important speech experience, and integrates drama with public speaking as well. Without a doubt, students will benefit greatly from this exercise. This method is not restricted to teachers of English or language arts, either. It is equally applicable to the social studies or science curriculum where a student could interview a historical figure or a famous scientist. That could be a very dynamic way to present content information to students.

CHAPTER FIVE

Effective Use of the Library

The school library offers the teacher two important resources. One is materials; the other is personnel. The latter may be either a librarian or an aide of some sort who is presumably knowledgeable about the resources of the library. The way you use your library probably depends on a number of different factors: what kind of collection it has, what type of program the librarian encourages, your own interest in and knowledge about different ways to use the library, and other facts that may be specific to your school. The library is a center where many resources and facilities, such as screen rooms, are available, generally to a large group. It is a valuable resource and an integral part of my program; I use it as much as possible.

Once the school year is underway and our classroom routines are reasonably set, I take time to introduce the library. As you may recall, I require my students to read one book every three weeks. So, at the beginning of each three-week interval, I set aside one class period to go to the library. At the library, I give a short book talk to acquaint students with certain authors or books they might want to consider reading. Then I give them the rest of the period to make their selections.

Let's take a closer look at how this works. I generally give the talk in the library not just with my class, but with one or two other teachers and their classes, all of whom will be choosing books. We are all there together because we have found that doing a library program as a team emphasizes the different strengths of the personnel involved. Each teacher has somewhat different expertise; while mine is books, another's may be films. Working together we can be more effective.

The students are seated for my presentation, but immediately after the talk, they will get up and look for books on the shelves. If I had given the book talk in my classroom, the walk to the library would have given many students the opportunity to forget everything I had told them.

Since my book report assignments usually specify the type of book the students must read, I always gear my talk around that category. I plan to talk for no more than ten or fifteen minutes, leaving students ample time to select books. I always begin with an introduction, so that my audience knows what to expect. I then talk about specific books that I have pulled from the shelves. It is important to have the books right there for the students to see. If I do a good job in my book talk, all the books I've pulled from the shelves will be checked out, as will any others I've mentioned.

During certain book talks, when we're starting a new quarter and thus a new category of book, I hand out a reading list on which I've listed appropriate books, for example survival books or World War II fiction. I tell my students to bear in mind that this is not a complete list, but it will give them someplace to start. On such lists, I am careful to include only books I know myself so that I avoid those my students would find less interesting. It's really important that I maintain my credibility with my students if they are to listen to any of my recommendations.

When I first established the book talk as a routine with my class, I discovered two things. First, I found that I had to read as many books as I could in order to constantly have new material to present. That was not a problem; I have thoroughly enjoyed that reading, and it has helped immensely in my goal of promoting reading with my students. My other discovery was the fact that we needed more books in the library. When I wanted to give a book talk on a particular author and we were missing half of the writer's books, I was a bit uncomfortable. I began looking for the books I wanted in paperback. Not only could we buy more books if we bought paperbacks instead of hardbacks, but many students already preferred paperbacks anyway, if only because they were easier to handle and carry.

This brings up an issue that you alone cannot decide: how to get more books into the library. The librarian has a budget and has likely spent that budget in a certain manner for some years. In an ideal situation, the librarian will be receptive to your suggestions or requests for certain titles. If so, be sure to check into different paperback distributors. Prices vary a great deal, and I have always been able to find a company with prices that were far lower than anyone else's.

If, on the other hand, you are unsuccessful in getting the titles you want onto the library order, you will need to consider other ways to add to the library collection. You might try going to other sources for money, such as the PTA, the student council, or community groups or businesses that are interested in education. This is always a good place to start. However, if no one gives you money to buy books, you can organize your own fund-raiser, or a book drive, or both.

A number of years ago, I discovered that many students had collections of books they had already read, which they were willing to give to the school. Consequently, I came up with the idea of a book drive. My class sponsored the drive, asking only for paperbacks. We specifically asked for books that would be appropriate for our library, which was used by fourth through eighth graders. We supplied a box to each class on which were attached directions, indicating the last day of the drive and when we would pick up the books. The class collecting the most books would win a prize.

During this book drive, which lasted one week, we collected over 400 books, 350 of which we carded for use in the library. They were in good condition, and many were exactly the books I had wanted the librarian to buy. We acquired books by Lois Duncan, Madeleine L'Engle, Katherine Paterson, Richard Peck, C. S. Lewis, and others too numerous to mention.

We accomplished several goals through the book drive. The most obvious was the addition of many good books to our library. In the process, we also impressed the librarian with our energy and efforts, especially since we carded all the books, saving her that time-consuming task. Another result of our efforts was a new recognition of how important the library was to all of us. The students realized that we had spent a lot of time doing something that benefited not only our class, but library users generally. We were proud of that. The students really enjoyed checking out the books that we had stamped as having been donated through our book drive. They all felt they had more of a stake in the library now, and what a great feeling that was!

Along with the book drive, we organized a fund-raiser to earn enough money to buy certain books that we knew would probably not be donated. We also paid for the prize for the winning class in the book drive out of the money we raised.

One reason I was able to be so successful in this project was the community in which I teach. Families in my area all buy books as well as supporting their libraries. This is obviously not the case everywhere. However, even if you teach in a less fortunate district, that does not mean that you will be unable to increase the collection of books in your library. You just need to go about it differently. First of all, you will need a source of funds. Again, this might be the PTA, the student council, or community groups or businesses; or you and your students can raise money yourselves, perhaps through sales of food, from bagels to cupcakes to packaged drinks, or through a car wash, or whatever form of fund-raising has traditionally worked for your school.

However you find the money, once you have it, you will want to organize a series of book-buying trips. What you accomplish with such trips is a valuable learning experience for your students, as well as the purchase of books for your library. By taking groups of students to a local bookstore, you give them the opportunity to browse in a place that is likely unfamiliar to them. Each student can be allowed to choose one paperback. Students may then take their chosen books home to read, and when they have finished, the books are donated to the library. This system is even more successful if the book is donated in the name of the student who chose it. You can show this by stamping the book or by using a bookplate.

Before making a book-buying trip, do some calling around to find a bookstore that will give you a discount, at least ten percent. Local businesses are often willing to provide this kind of service in exchange for a mention of their good deed in your school newsletter. Perhaps you could get your librarian to help you with this type of program. He or she might even be willing to take students to the bookstore on buying trips. But even if you must do it all by yourself, the benefits of such a program are certainly worth the time and effort you will expend.

After our own very successful book drive, our next library project was a bulletin board. We felt that an attractive display would not only enhance the appearance of the library, but could also aid students in selecting books. The librarian was more than willing to allow me and my class to put up and maintain such a bulletin board.

For our display, we used a large piece of fadeless paper for the background and framed it in yarn. Then we cut out letters saying *GOOD BOOKS*. Once this basic frame was up, we stapled envelopes along the bottom of the bulletin board to hold book recommendation cards, which I explain in detail in chapter 6. To complete the display, we posted selected student book reports, both art and written. In addition to being very attractive, the bulletin board caught the students' attention, as they always enjoyed seeing each other's work on display. We hoped it would serve its purpose, to give students ideas of good books they might want to read; and, in fact, it has.

To guarantee that the bulletin board would change every three weeks, we decided to assign someone to take care of it. It became a student responsibility. Now all I have to do is collect materials I want to see on the bulletin board in a box that is so marked. Then the student whose job it is can take those items and redo the display for each new three-week period. This student responsibility rotates throughout the year.

The bulletin board is useful to the librarian, as well. She uses it especially with students who are in classes with nonreading teachers. Since the bulletin board and the book recommendation cards are changed every three weeks, they offer a constant source of new information for the librarian.

Of course, you cannot ignore the fact that the librarian is going to be greatly affected by all of the increased activity in the library. In our school the librarian's main goal is, perhaps, helping students find books they will enjoy. Since the students in my classes become even more eager readers as the year goes by, the librarian's job becomes both more pleasant and more challenging. My best readers, especially eighth graders, tend to "read out" or exhaust the library. She must help them find other good books to read, and she must buy more books that will appeal to these avid readers. As a result of my program, she also finds that students now like particular authors, and they want the library to stock copies of *all* the books these authors have written. When students themselves ask for books, it seems to have an especially strong impact on the librarian, for she really does want to offer the books that they want to read.

The librarian in my school has also begun a practice that helps her and benefits good readers at the same time. When a new shipment of books arrives, she asks several good readers to preview the books for her. Students are delighted to be given such an important job, and the librarian is relieved not to have to read all those books herself, a task she probably couldn't complete anyway. Using this method, she gets some idea of what the new books are like, and she also has a valuable resource in the student who previewed the book for her. That student becomes an "authority" to whom she can send others when they want to know more about a certain book.

So far I have talked only about the most obvious library resource—books. However, another library resource you shouldn't forget is the film offering. There are a number of films based on books that offer us a good comparison between the two media. One example is *The Tap Dance Kid*, a movie made from Louise Fitzhugh's book, *Nobody's Family Is Going to Change*. Though the movie and book differ in some respects, the filmmakers were basically true to Fitzhugh's story.

The film *Snowbound* is based on Harry Mazer's book of the same name. The film is not as effective as the book, being weakened by an attempt to make it funnier and more frightening than the novel itself. The novel seems more realistic than the film, and the contrast is an excellent lesson for a class.

The film version of *A Separate Peace*, based on John Knowles' book, is excellent. It moves along more quickly than the novel, and the actors do a fine job of portraying their characters.

All of these films, and many others, are available through county film libraries or community libraries that lend films. Showing them in class can enhance your reading program, expanding your students' understanding of the differences that arise in telling a story on paper and showing it on film.

In summary, I view the library as an extension of my classroom and I use it as such. I am comfortable there, and I want all of my students to feel likewise. Such class projects as the book drive and the bulletin board serve to increase student familiarity with the library. Consequently, many students now share my attitude that the library is an important part of our school.

CHAPTER SIX

Book Recommendation Cards

Some of my students know exactly what they want to read all the time, but others need guidance. The book recommendation card is one good way to help students find books that they will enjoy, perhaps the best way to provide information on good books when you can't be there yourself. The cards are placed in special envelopes on a bulletin board, either in the library or in your classroom. They are then available to students whenever they need some new ideas for outside reading.

I have my students fill out the cards on books they have enjoyed reading for book reports. There is no point, I tell them, in filling out a card on a book you wouldn't recommend. Included on the card is a space to write the category into which the book falls, such as mystery, science fiction, biography, fantasy, animals, the supernatural, historical fiction, and so forth.

In addition to such basic data as the title, author, and category of the book, I ask students to write information in three major areas: a brief discussion of the main character, a little bit about the story line, and the reader's reasons for recommending this particular book. I also have students include their own names on the cards as the reviewers. That way, if someone is intrigued but would like to find out a little more about the book, he or she knows whom to ask.

In order to ensure that the information on the cards will be carefully done, I have found that I must make the book recommendation cards a specific assignment. I first hand out a form that the students will use for writing their rough drafts. It duplicates the format I put on the actual card, but I run it off on ditto paper instead. After they finish their rough drafts, I can read their work and make suggestions for corrections or changes. Students can then carefully copy their final work on prepared, 5 × 8 index cards. The goal is to produce book recommendation cards that are clear, informative, and easy to read, as well as being mechanically correct.

```
┌─────────────────────────────────────────────────────┐
│                                                       │
│  Book Recommendation Card      _____      │
│                                      title            │
│          _____              _____      │
│            category                  author           │
│                                  _____      │
│  Main character + brief description:  reviewer        │
│                                                       │
│                                                       │
│  .                                                    │
│  Basic story line:                                    │
│                                                       │
│                                                       │
│  Recommendation:                                      │
│                                                       │
│                                                       │
└─────────────────────────────────────────────────────┘
```

For this assignment, I advise giving the class a certain amount of instruction, at least the first time they do the recommendation cards. After that, a brief review might be all they need, especially if you ask them to complete a rough draft.

The difficult part is learning how to get enough good information into a relatively small space and have it still be readable and make sense. You might provide some sample cards for students to study. These could be recommendations that you have written yourself, or some you have elicited from the class and written on the board in the proper format. Regardless of your method, keep your goal in mind: clear, useful recommendation cards!

You will need to talk with students about what to write for each section of the card, and how to write it most efficiently in the small space. The first section deals with the main character. What we are interested in reading here is a brief description of the protagonist—who that person is, what that person does, what kind of person he or she is, and so forth. Students need to learn how to select their words carefully to get the maximum amount of information from the fewest words. For example, if the main character is a young boy who lives on a farm, he should be referred to as a *farm boy* (two words) rather than as a *boy who lives on a farm* (six words). Normally, students don't pay much attention to saying things so succinctly, but in this assignment, that skill is very important.

The second section on the card deals with the basic story line. Here the student should write several sentences that explain where the character is and what that character is doing or is about to do. Students must understand that we have no desire to read a complete story summary. That would not suit the purpose of a recommendation card, nor would it fit in the allotted space. Once again, brevity really needs to be emphasized.

The third section of the card is left for the student's recommendation. Here we want the student to tell us why we would like the book. A student might indicate whether the book will keep us in suspense, make us laugh or cry, scare us, or affect us in some other way. This is a good place to explain if this is a book in a series, especially if it's not the first. If the book is particularly difficult to read, that too might be noted.

Following is an example of how the information reads on a good book recommendation card. The book is *Summer of the Monkeys* by Wilson Rawls; the category is adventure.

Main Character and Brief Description. Jay Berry is an 11-year-old boy who loves to hunt with his dog, Rowdy. He is curious and persistent and has a grandfather with similar qualities.

Basic Story Line. A boy encounters a tree full of monkeys in a river bottom in the Ozark Mountains. This leads to a tragedy as well as an unusual summer for him.

Recommendation. This book will make you laugh and cry, but, above all, you will want to keep reading to find out how Jay Berry deals with that tree full of monkeys.

Once the cards are completed, I sort them as to category, then slip each set into the corresponding envelope on the library bulletin board. If there are duplicates for any book, I file only one. Each time we fill out cards, usually once every three weeks, we change the library files. From one time to the next, certain cards might be left in the envelope if they provide information that hasn't been duplicated by anyone else.

Although I generally assign the book recommendation cards at regular intervals, sometimes I may not want to spend the class time necessary to have the students fill them out. However, I still may want students to share the titles of good books they've been reading. To this end, I ask anyone who has read a praiseworthy book to write just the title, the author, the category, and his or her own name on a 3 × 5 card. Then I post those cards on our classroom bulletin board for easy reference. While they don't provide the detailed information of the book recommendation card, they do offer students some titles to consider.

The envelopes for filing the book recommendation cards should be sturdy enough to last all year. We make ours out of file folders that we cut and tape at the sides. If you cut the back piece one inch higher than the front, there is room to staple or tack the envelope to the bulletin board where it is easily accessible. Use a marking pen to write one category of book on the front of each envelope. The diagram shows how I turn a letter-size folder into two of these envelopes.

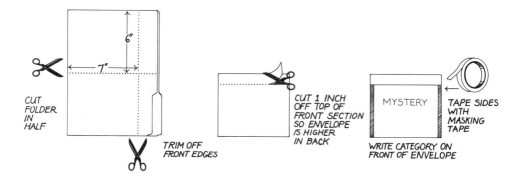

CUT FOLDER IN HALF

6″

7″

TRIM OFF FRONT EDGES

CUT 1 INCH OFF TOP OF FRONT SECTION SO ENVELOPE IS HIGHER IN BACK

MYSTERY

WRITE CATEGORY ON FRONT OF ENVELOPE

TAPE SIDES WITH MASKING TAPE

The use of book recommendation cards, filed in envelopes on the library bulletin board, accomplishes several purposes. First, your students complete a writing assignment on a book they have read—an assignment that requires them to be very specific. Such writing practice is always valuable. Second, the cards are available to your students to assist them in choosing books for your outside reading program. If a student wants to read a mystery, for example, the bulletin board display will provide cards for ten or more mysteries that fellow students have recommended. Additionally, students in other classes can use these cards. The system may even become an organized, schoolwide program. And finally, the placement of the book recommendation cards in the library draws more people there, which is a real bonus. All my students have benefited from the addition of book recommendation cards to my program.

CHAPTER SEVEN

A Classroom Paperback Collection

In any school, the central library is going to be the major source of books, it being eminently sensible to have them all in one place. However, an individual classroom library can also be a very positive resource. This way, the books are right there in the classroom where your students are, making it very convenient for the students to check them out. A classroom library can also be more specialized, containing only books that you particularly like and feel your students would enjoy—in other words, no duds.

Starting a classroom library is very simple. All you need to do is take a few paperbacks that are appropriate for your students and put them on a shelf marked *Classroom Library*. You should devise a check-out system so that you will not lose your books.

The check-out system can be as simple as a sign-up sheet that includes a space for the student's name and the book title. When the student returns the book, his or her name is crossed out. If you don't feel that this system will be successful, you can card each of the books, the way a regular library does. To check out a book, the student signs and dates the card, which you then keep in a box. Establish a time limit for keeping the books. Check the cards in the box weekly and encourage students, by name, to return the books that are due. It is wise to keep a list of all the books you have in your library, if for nothing else than to let students know what is available. You are bound to lose some books, as all libraries do, but I find that if you check on the students periodically, you will be able to keep your classroom library books circulating nicely.

There are numerous ways to build up a collection of books. If you order books for your students through a book club, the club will often send you several books free, depending on the size of your order. If you shop at a second-hand store, you will find shelves of used paperbacks that are priced very cheaply. While you must be selective, some of these will certainly be suitable for your students. If you frequent garage sales or library book sales, you will be able to pick up even more books at very reasonable prices. To pay for these books, you might ask for funds to support your program; if that doesn't work, you can pay for them yourself—the cost is tax deductible. Whatever methods you use to put together your collection of books, once you have them, you ought to *do* something with them.

It's a good idea to set up your classroom library bookshelf in a place that is easily accessible. The best type is a free-standing shelf that can be moved. This way, you can start out with it near a bulletin board that features the classroom library, probably in September when you are acquainting your students with classroom routines and resources. Make it clear that the classroom library is available specifically for their use. They should all know where it is, what it includes, and how to use it. Later, when you feel the students no longer need to be reminded of the library shelf, you can move it to a more convenient location.

If you cannot get a movable shelf, find an area in the classroom that is easy to use and nonintimidating. Ideally, there might be a desk or table by the bookshelf—or even a rug and pillows—so that students could sit down comfortably to browse through the books. The books should be kept in alphabetical order, by author, so that students can find what they are looking for easily. You might want to appoint a student librarian to be sure the shelf is kept neat and in order.

Even if you are not convinced that a classroom library is particularly important, I beg you to consider trying one anyway. Over the years, I have lent my own books to many students, not just those in my classes, but other teachers' students as well. As a result, I have had many wonderful opportunities to talk about books with these young people. One book that I have lent to many students is *Eric* by Doris Lund. This is the biography of a boy who is dying of leukemia, written by the boy's mother. It is a fascinating and very well-written story. During the quarters when my students are required to read nonfiction, *Eric* is checked out by many students. When I lend a book, I always ask the reader about it when it is returned. Most students have liked the book *Eric*, but their remarks are generally about the character rather than the book itself. For example, a student will remark how brave *Eric* was or how sad it was that such a nice boy had to die. We often go on to talk about the humorous anecdotes in the book—in many cases, their inclusion surprises the students, who forget that life can be funny even when it's full of problems. Other students, overhearing such a conversation, will often decide to read the book, too. This is where having the classroom library is a real bonus; the book is right there and can be checked out immediately, before the student has a chance to forget about it.

I do want to caution you, though, not to think of a classroom library as a substitute for the school or public library. It is not. Every student should learn to use and enjoy the main library. None of us would ever want our students to restrict their reading to what we can hand them in the classroom.

One final note on the use of a classroom library: students must be expected to handle the books carefully. No one wants to read a paperback with the cover torn off or the pages excessively dog-eared. Standards must be set and followed, with penalties for abuse if that seems necessary.

Although my classroom library was embarrassingly small when I first set it up, it has grown into a good-sized collection. I add to it whenever possible, and I feel that it contributes something special to my classroom. It makes certain popular books readily available for students to borrow; it also provides me with books to discuss in my early book talks. Perhaps most important, it provides a natural environment where I can engage students in pleasant conversations about books and reading—one more way to encourage the sharing that is such a fundamental part of my program.

CHAPTER EIGHT

Results

Now that I've shared with you the methods I use to interest my students in outside reading and to encourage them to read more, let me explain what I observe each year in June that convinces me I'm doing the right thing. First of all, by the end of the year everyone has read twelve books for book reports. I have recorded the titles and authors of those books on each student's reading record form as the year goes along, so by June, the students can be proud of how much they have actually read. This feeling of accomplishment, plus a clear interest in reading, can be sensed in their conversation during book-selection periods in the fourth quarter. A student will remark to me that he particularly enjoyed a book by John Christopher that he read during the first quarter, so now he's decided to read a second book by that author. Another student will mention to me that the Lois Duncan book she has wanted to read is finally in, so now she can check it out. Yet another student will comment to me that he is going to read a certain Harry Harrison book over the summer because one of his classmates is going to lend it to him. None of these comments is artificial. They are all sincere remarks, made by students who have become much more involved in reading than they were at the beginning of the year. They are genuinely interested in books. This is exactly what I hoped would happen.

Besides talking to *me* about the books they've read and the books they might read, students also now talk to *each other* about the same things, both in the library and in the halls. This is often a direct result of something in my program. Suppose Scott has given a book talk, written a book recommendation card, or done a book report on a title that Jessica is interested in. Jessica will likely seek out Scott, who already read the book, in order to get more information. This often results in the students looking for the particular book together, or even one student lending a book to the other. I like to make the most of such sharing among peers, so I will sometimes specifically send one student to talk with another who has read a book I feel the first student will also enjoy.

During the last weeks of school, I post a large piece of paper headed *Summer Reading.* Students may write on this sheet the title and author of any books they feel should appear on our summer reading list. Obviously, anyone who is truly enjoying books will want to continue reading during the summer. Since I have been providing reading guidance in many forms all year long, I feel it is important to put together a summer reading list to continue that guidance. The list serves a dual purpose. It not only provides information for the student, it also encourages the student to continue to read. The recommendation list includes some specific titles, as well as the names of many authors who have written lots of good books. Although I don't want to spend a lot of time indicating the reading level of the books on the list, I do want to help the students choose books at appropriate difficulty levels. Therefore, I mark each of the titles as easy, medium, or hard. I talk about these levels a bit at the end of the year, giving examples of books my students know so that they will understand the labels. This simple system seems to work perfectly well.

As the year ends, I always express the hope that, in September, students will come back to share with me their reactions to books they've read during the summer. I often mention books that I plan to read myself, and I ask the class what titles they intend to read. This gives students a mental set that can be helpful when they get far away from school, not thinking about the intellectual side of life. Each September, I am generally very pleased with the amount of reading my students have done. They do come to talk with me about certain books, and that leads right into the new school year with evidence that my goal has been met: my students *do* read more and enjoy it.

I want to leave with you the very strong belief that you *can* affect the reading habits of your students. They will respond to your efforts to get them to read more, but you must first make a commitment yourself. You must be a fine role model for them. It is not enough to talk; you must act on your conviction that reading is a wonderfully satisfying activity that everyone should embrace wholeheartedly. Your students will want to know what you have read, and once they believe that you are an avid reader, they too will take steps in that direction.

APPENDIX

Recommended Reading

To help you get started reading, I have included in this appendix a list of authors for you to consider, plus five separate book lists: survival fiction; World War II fiction; mystery and suspense; supernatural, timewarp, and fantasy books; and general fiction. Notice that I say "to help *you* get started reading." These lists are designed for *you*, not your classes. This is in line with my philosophy that if you expect your students to read, it is essential that you have read *their* books, essential that you be able to share your impressions with them.

You don't think it's necessary? Perhaps several examples will help to illustrate my line of thinking. If you were overweight and came to my fitness center to be guided to a new and thinner shape, you might have some difficulty remaining committed to your goal if I weighed in at a hefty 300 pounds. Somehow, what I *said* would be undermined by what I *was*! Likewise, if you decided to give up smoking and came to my seminar designed to help you quit, your belief in my system might be shaken a bit when you saw me light up during a break.

In guiding students to books and authors, we all have more credibility if we have read them ourselves, if we can converse about them, if we can share. That is why I first began to read "kid lit." Now, you can't keep me away from the adolescent novel.

Where do you start? Try my recommended author list first. Once you are acquainted with several of these authors, you are on your way. I suggest that you start with authors who have written many books with varying reading levels. Zilpha Snyder is a good example. Her novels, including *The Velvet Room*, *The Egypt Game*, and *Witches of Worm*, are excellent for fourth- to seventh-grade readers, while her fantasy/science-fiction series, beginning with *Below the Root*, is very good but more challenging. Read anything by Zilpha Snyder, and you will know at least a little about an author who has written many books and to whom you can refer a variety of students. Katherine Paterson and Paul Gallico are similar in this respect. Paterson's *The Great Gilly Hopkins* and *Bridge to Terabithia* are good for younger readers, while *Rebels of the Heavenly Kingdom* and other titles set in the Orient are much more advanced. Paul Gallico wrote the charming book *Thomasina: The Cat Who Thought She Was God*, as well as *The Boy with the Bubble Gun* and the tense and dramatic *The Poseidon Adventure*. For the individual titles in the five book lists that follow, I have coded the books *E, M,* or *H* to indicate *easy, medium,* or *hard* reading. This assessment is based on my subjective impression of the books and how students of different reading levels have reacted to them.

Once you have started reading, keep track of the books you read so that you can include them on book lists, refer to them in book talks, and recommend them to individual students. In my records, I note the title, author, category, reading level, and a short comment about the book, including my reaction to it. I often refer to these notes, and they usually tell me enough that I don't need to refer back to the books themselves.

Once I had begun reading "kid lit," I was so intrigued by the variety and the quality that I began to regard it, not as "school work," but as one more aspect of my pleasure reading. I also found myself having such wonderful conversations with my students that any thought of *not* reading young people's literature fled from my mind. I'm convinced that my reading has brought a new dimension to my language arts program. As the saying goes, "Try it, you'll like it!"

RECOMMENDED AUTHORS

Adams, Richard
Ames, Mildred
Angell, Judi
Beagle, Peter
Bethancourt, T. Ernesto
Bonham, Frank
Cameron, Eleanor
Chant, Joy
Christie, Agatha
Christopher, John
Clapp, Patricia
Conford, Ellen
Cooper, Susan
Corcoran, Barbara
Danziger, Paula
Duncan, Lois
Gallico, Paul
George, Jean
Greene, Bette

Harrison, Harry
Hinton, S. E.
Kerr, Judith
Kerr, M. E.
L'Engle, Madeleine
Nixon, Jean Lowery
Paterson, Katherine
Peck, Richard
Pinkwater, D. M.
Raskin, Ellen
Roberts, Willo Davis
Snyder, Zilpha
Stewart, Mary
Taylor, Mildred
Taylor, Theodore
Thrasher, Crystal
Tolan, Stephanie
Tolkien, J. R. R.
Wibberley, Leonard

SURVIVAL FICTION BOOK LIST

Burnford, Sheila. **The Incredible Journey.** E–M

Most survival stories are about people who experience hardships. This story tells of two dogs and a cat who, while trying to find their master, encounter great difficulties and danger. By banding together and helping each other, they do very well on a difficult journey. This is a wonderful book that everyone enjoys.

Christopher, John. **Fireball.** M

Brad and Simon, two English teenagers, are mysteriously transported back to an earlier time, hundreds of years ago, when Britain was under Roman rule. Latin is spoken; horses provide transportation; life is rather primitive. As the two boys learn how to survive in this different world, they become involved in a rather scary series of events.

Cooper, Susan. **Seaward.** H

Some years ago I read a series by Cooper, starting with *Over Sea Under Stone*, which I adored. The story had elements of both mystery and fantasy, with interesting characters as well as unusual situations. This new book is equally engaging. West and Cally meet when both are experiencing grief, and they confront difficulties that greatly test them. The two proceed from their own world into strange lands where they have odd and frightening encounters. Together they must learn to be brave as well as kind and trusting. In their struggles to survive, West and Cally learn to count on other people as well as to distrust certain individuals. The book is fascinating—good reading for a good reader.

Ellis, Mel. **The Wild Horse Killers.** M

Living on a ranch and growing up in the west, Sandra Bradford loves and appreciates animals and the environment where they live. When she discovers that her own horse, a red stallion, has joined a herd of wild mustangs that are being rounded up by wild horse killers, she decides to do something about it. Sandra's mission is exciting and dangerous. Her story reminds the reader of the wonders of our wilderness and the need to keep it free. I liked this book!

George, Jean Craighead. **The Talking Earth.** M

You may know this author's two other fine survival novels, *My Side of the Mountain* and *Julie of the Wolves*. Once again, George has written a good story about a person surviving on her own. Billie Wind is a Seminole Indian girl who is skeptical of many of her elder's beliefs. To test those beliefs, she goes off into the Florida Everglades to see for herself whether the Earth and the animals and birds talk. Her experiences, including a devastating fire that is followed a bit later by a hurricane, give her a good opportunity to listen to the animals and the birds. She discovers that they have a great deal to tell her. Billie Wind is a fine character whose story makes good reading.

Greenberg, Jan. **No Dragons to Slay.** H

Although this is not a difficult book to read, it is definitely written for a more mature reader than most adolescent novels. The main character is a high school junior when he finds out that he has a cancerous tumor. Thomas's experiences are grim ones, beginning with his fear of dying and continuing with his distress at going bald, the reaction of other people to his situation, and the nausea he suffers after chemotherapy. His story makes clear that it's not easy having cancer, even if you are planning to recover from it. Thomas meets a young woman, a friend of his mother, who helps him in ways his own parents and his teachers haven't. Ultimately, she gets him involved in an archaeology project, which turns out to be fun as well as eye-opening for Thomas in terms of the other teenagers he meets there. This book is a good one, but for a generally more mature reader than you might have in seventh or eighth grade.

Judson, William. **Cold River.** M

Lizzy and Tim go with their father on an October canoe trip, which is planned to last about ten days. They intend to go down Beaver Creek but instead end up in Cold River. That is where a decision makes a real difference in their lives: they decide to continue down Cold River. When they run into rapids, their canoe overturns and the father's leg is broken. The children are safe, but they are unable to nurse their father back to health.

He catches pneumonia and dies. Now the children are faced with figuring out how to survive on their own. The story is exciting and gives the reader much information on surviving in the wilderness.

Langford, Sondra Gordon. **Red Bird of Ireland.**   M

One of the driest subjects in school may be social studies, because we tend to teach events rather than the people who lived them. In this novel, Langford writes a charming story about the terrible famine in Ireland. The reader has the opportunity to see history unfold as it is lived by Aderyn Moynihan, her family, and the rest of the people who live in her town. These are people who work as tenant farmers for a wealthy lord. Eventually, when they are unable to pay their rent, the lord ships them off to the New World. We see the starvation, sickness, and general deprivation these people face, but their spirits remain unbroken. It is a good story, told well.

Mazer, Harry. **Snowbound.**   E

Because Tony's family won't let him keep a dog he brings home, he throws a fit and takes the family car, not sure where he's going. It's January and bound to be wintery in Upper New York State where Tony lives. He picks up a hitchhiker, Cindy, and the two of them have an amazing adventure. They are lucky to get out of it alive. Mazer has written a good story about survival as well as about helping others, not just yourself.

Smith, Rukshana. **Sumitra's Story.**   H

This novel is very revealing of the nature of families in different cultures and how their customs and expectations affect their children when they move to a new country whose customs and expectations are different. Sumitra and her family are from India, but they reside in Uganda. When the policy of Africanization is established, the family is no longer welcome in Africa, so they move to England. Here Sumitra discovers that her family's way of life is quite different from that of English families. Sumitra spends a number of years in school and then working, trying to decide how *she* will live her life. Her parents have already decided what is best for her, but Sumitra no longer accepts their ideas. This causes a struggle that makes good reading for an eager reader.

Taylor, Theodore. **Teetoncey.**   E–M

> Ben O'Neal is an 11-year-old boy who lives on an island off of
> North Carolina, where the focus of life is the sea. When a stormy
> night results in a shipwreck, Ben's life is significantly changed.
> He and his mother take in the only survivor of the wreck, a girl
> who first seems half dead and later clearly suffers from amne-
> sia. This first book of the Cape Hatteras trilogy is a good mys-
> tery and adventure, as are the next two books, *Teetoncey and
> Ben O'Neal* and *The Odyssey of Ben O'Neal*. Taylor, also author
> of *The Cay*, is a fine storyteller.

Zalben, Jane Breskin. **Maybe It Will Rain Tomorrow.**   M

> The subject of suicide is a rare one in adolescent novels, even
> though the statistics tell us that quite a few teenagers take their
> own lives. In this novel, Beth Corey finds her mother dead of
> an overdose one morning. Beth, shocked and terribly upset, is
> forced to pack up and go to live with her father and his new
> wife, with their baby, on Long Island. At the age of 16, Beth
> knows it is going to be difficult getting used to new people and
> places; but making such a change knowing she will never see
> her mother again is particularly distressing to her. Zalben does
> a fine job of creating a three-dimensional teenage character
> who develops and changes, just as the characters in adult nov-
> els do. This book deals very well with a difficult subject.

Other books to consider:

Bonham, Frank. **Durango Street; Devilhorn; Gimme an H, Gimme
    an E, Gimme an L, Gimme a P.**

Cormier, Robert. **The Chocolate War; After the First Death; Now
    and at the Hour.**

Hinton, S. E. **The Outsiders; Rumble Fish; Tex.**

WORLD WAR II FICTION BOOK LIST

Allen, Mabel Esther. **A Dream of Hunger Moss.**   M

This book has an intriguing setting: the English countryside near a boggy area called the Moss. It is the late 1930s, and World War II is not far away. Alice and Adam get to know this area when their mother must have an operation and time to recuperate. She sends them to stay with old friends, Mr. and Mrs. Farmer, who live on a farm near the Moss. She herself had stayed with the Farmers as a child and remembers them and their home fondly. It is almost as though Alice relives her mother's experiences, and they are rather unusual. The book is reasonably good.

Arnold, Elliott. **A Kind of Secret Weapon.**   E–M

One of the elements of life for people living in Nazi-occupied countries during World War II was the underground newspaper. This story tells of just such an operation in Denmark, in which Peter Andersen and his family are involved as part of the Danish Resistance. Not only is the story a captivating one, it also shows to what lengths people will go to fight oppression. This is an important aspect of the study of World War II.

Bauer, Marion Dane. **Rain of Fire.**   M

I have read a lot of World War II fiction, and most of it deals with people's experiences while the war is going on. This novel takes place after Matthew comes home from the war and doesn't manage very well. His 12-year-old brother Steve doesn't understand his silence, his inability to get a job, and his attitude about the war. Neither do his parents. In fact, the whole town is embarrassed that Matthew feels sorry for the Japanese in Hiroshima where he was part of the American occupation forces. A prank in which Steve is involved prompts Matthew to talk about his experiences in Japan, and finally Steve begins to understand Matthew's feelings. This is a good story, valuable for its impressions of how people felt after the end of World War II.

Cooper, Susan. **Dawn of Fear.**   E

Derek, Geoff, and Peter are ordinary boys who happen to live in England while World War II is being fought. As German planes fly overhead on their way to London, the boys gaze at them in fascination. They even cheer the RAF planes that chase them. War doesn't seem to affect their lives until air raids become more frequent and the adults around them become more and more nervous. This book does a good job of showing how World War II intruded on the lives of common people.

Corcoran, Barbara. **Axe-Time, Sword-Time.**   M–H

Elinor Golden was hit in the head by a golf ball when she was a child, and the accident left her brain slightly damaged. This made learning more difficult for her. We meet Elinor when she is in high school, very discouraged about her future. Her family always expected her to do well in school, and she feels she's a real disappointment to them. It happens to be the early 1940s, and World War II is being fought. When Elinor's brother and boyfriend go off to fight, she feels rather useless staying at home. Eventually, Elinor gets a job as an inspector for the Navy and finally feels that she is helping in the war effort as well as becoming independent. This is a good story offering insights into the effect of the war on Americans who stayed home.

Ferry, Charles. **Raspberry One.**   M

Ferry does a good job of showing us real people who lived through the worst aspects of World War II. Nick and Hildy, two young American men, will soon be shipped off to the Pacific where they will fly bombing raids against the Japanese. Before they go, they meet two young women and fall in love. Together they all have a wonderful time, but the war looms, and the two must finally ship out. The war scenes are particularly believable. They aren't pretty, but they certainly are realistic. This is a fine story in a believable setting.

Greene, Bette. **Summer of My German Soldier.**   H

Patty Bergen was bored the summer that German prisoners were held in a POW camp built outside her town of Jenkinsville, Arkansas. Patty was a very intelligent girl who was not at all appreciated by her family. They thought she was too plain looking and asked too many questions. The first person who truly appreciated Patty's intelligence and curiosity was Anton, an escaped German soldier. Patty concealed him in the room above the family garage, which was her hideaway. Once Patty met Anton, her life was never to be the same again. This is the first novel in a two-part series, well-written with a compelling plot. I loved it! The second book is called *Morning Is a Long Time Coming*.

Kerr, Judith. **When Hitler Stole Pink Rabbit; The Other Way Round; A Small Person Far Away.** M

Kerr has written a series that follows the Schmidt family from Germany to Switzerland, then to France, and finally to England. It is the mid 1930s, and just before Hitler is elected, the Schmidts depart for Switzerland where they will stay until they learn if they can return safely to Germany. Herr Schmidt is a writer, and he is convinced that he will not be free to write under Hitler's rule. Unfortunately he is right, and the Schmidts become refugees. The books read particularly well. They show that moving to a new place is generally an adventure for Max and Anna, the children, but a real burden for their parents. Few American teenagers understand the concept of being refugees, but it is possible for them to get an idea of what it's like by reading about the Schmidt family. This is an excellent series dealing with World War II.

Mazer, Harry. **The Last Mission.** M

War is romantic, right? That is certainly what 15-year-old Jack Raab thinks about World War II, which is being fought overseas in Europe. Jack wants to be involved in all that glamour, and he manages to make it happen by using his older brother's birth certificate to enlist in the Army. Jack eventually becomes a gunner and sees far more action than he ever wanted to. This is a very realistic story about the everyday events of war.

Sachs, Marilyn. **A Pocket Full of Seeds.** M

Nicole Nieman is a French girl who finds her life drastically altered by World War II. The first changes she notices involve having less food, a disturbing attitude of certain people toward Jews, and a general feeling of fear. Eventually, Nicole's mother, father, and sister are arrested and taken to prison, though she doesn't know where. The only person who will take Nicole in is a teacher who houses the girl in the school dormitory and forges papers for her. Nicole has no idea if she'll ever see her family again. Marilyn Sachs based this novel on a true story. It reads very well.

Uchida, Yoshiko. **Journey to Topaz** and **Journey Home.**   E–M

The relocation of Japanese-Americans in 1942 is part of our country's World War II history. It happened, even though most Americans may wish it hadn't. In these two books, Uchida tells the story of a Berkeley, California family that is relocated to a camp in Utah called Topaz. Their lives in the camp are stark by contrast to how they lived earlier. When they are released, they find it extremely difficult to return home and find housing, work, and peace of mind. Uchida herself was relocated to just such a camp and has done a fine job of telling the story of what happened to those who endured this painful experience.

Other books to consider:

Joffo, Joseph. **A Bag of Marbles.**

Leffland, Ella. **Rumors of Peace.**

Walsh, Jill Paton. **Fire Weed.**

Westall, Robert. **The Machine Gunners.**

MYSTERY AND SUSPENSE BOOK LIST

Bethancourt, T. Ernesto. **Doris Fein: Deadly Aphrodite.** M

I always look to see if Bethancourt has another Doris Fein book out, and if he does, I know I'll be highly entertained by another good mystery. In *Deadly Aphrodite*, Doris discovers that an exclusive health spa uses questionable techniques to "help" clients look better. Doris herself is helped to new slimness, but she is a wreck afterwards. This leads her to investigate the spa. I always enjoy brash Doris Fein who is determined to be treated as an individual, not as a girl or an inexperienced young woman. She succeeds, every time, in keeping me entertained.

Dicks, Terrance. **The Case of the Missing Masterpiece.** E

It is such fun to read about amateurs solving a crime, perhaps because I wish I could do so myself. The situations in which four teenagers find themselves here are fascinating as well as scary. Their leader, Dan Robinson, decides to try to solve a crime after a classmate makes fun of his interest in Sherlock Holmes. When Dan and three friends try applying Holmes's methods to this case, they are in for some excitement.

Holland, Isabelle. **Perdita.** M

A girl who calls herself Perdita Smith is suffering from amnesia as a result of a fall. She has been staying at a convent to recover, but now she must go out and *do* things to increase the chances of recovering her memory. Since she feels that she knows something about horses, she gets a job at a riding stable. There she begins to regain her memory, but in odd bits and pieces with a great deal missing. It is clear that some of what Perdita is going to remember is frightening, perhaps best left alone. The story is a terrific one for horse lovers as well as those who enjoy a good mystery. Holland includes several intriguing characters in addition to Perdita. I couldn't put this book down!

Holland, Isabelle. **Trelawny.** H

This is a Gothic novel for teenagers, with all the suspense and mystery one expects from this type of story. Kit Trelawny inherits a mansion in which her ancestors had lived for years. She had been there once as a child, when she and her mother had been royally snubbed by the reigning Trelawnys. Now that she owns the sprawling mansion, she decides to turn it into an artists' colony. The adventure she falls into while trying to do this is very exciting. I was hooked.

Johnston, Norma. **Gabriel's Girl.** M

This author tells an intriguing and complicated mystery of international crime. Sarah Langham, the main character, tries to solve a mystery involving her father. He has disappeared, and Sarah feels that he is in danger. All kinds of amazing things happen once Sarah flies to Spain to unravel the mystery surrounding her father's disappearance. I found the story riveting.

Kidd, Ronald. **Sizzle & Splat.** E

This story is funny, mysterious, and thoroughly enjoyable. Two members of a youth orchestra decide to investigate an unusual mystery surrounding their orchestra and its need for funds. They get involved in quite a plot; in fact, they almost get in over their heads, but they always are able to laugh at their situation, and the reader enjoys even more laughs.

Klaveness, Jan O'Donnell. **The Griffin Legacy.** M

When Amy Enfield has to stay with her grandmother until her parents get settled, she is not sure she'll be happy. What she doesn't know is that she's going to have the adventure of her life. Amy's grandmother and great-aunt live in an old house in Massachusetts, in an area where the Revolutionary War was fought. Memories of that period abound. Amy becomes acquainted with legends of the past and eventually tries to solve the mystery surrounding one of those legends. This is a very good story, both scary and filled with suspense.

MacLeod, Charlotte. **Cirak's Daughter.** M

A good mystery is such fun, and this one is quite good. I genuinely felt afraid for Jenny, the 19-year-old who inherits a lot of money from the father who had deserted her and her mother seventeen years earlier. When Jenny tries to discover details of her father's life, she becomes enmeshed in some rather mysterious events. The entire story is very satisfying.

L'Engle, Madeleine. **The Arm of the Starfish.**   H

In this novel, L'Engle puts a young man who has just graduated from high school into a very difficult situation. Adam Eddington is flying to Spain to work for the summer for a scientist who has a lab on an island called Gaea. Before he even gets there, he is drawn into a power struggle that is very complicated and definitely beyond his comprehension. Adam finds himself unclear as to which side is good and which is bad. It is very exciting to find out, along with Adam, just what is going on. This book reads well but is for a good reader.

Lyle, Katie Letcher. **Finders Weepers.**   H

Lee Eldridge lives in Virginia with her mother, father, and two brothers. She is a practical girl, voted "Most Sensible" by her eighth-grade class, an honor she is not so sure about. She spends the summer with her grandmother and uncle in a very small town called Lavesia, Virginia. This particular summer she finds a treasure that is intriguing, upsetting, and dangerous all at once. Lee's experiences provide a real adventure for the reader, too.

Nixon, Joan Lowery. **A Deadly Game of Magic.**   M

This book scared me. Four high school students are on their way home from a drama contest when their car breaks down in a bad storm. They take shelter in a house that they come upon in the middle of nowhere. There, they encounter someone who seems to be trying very hard to scare them out of their wits. They can't see the person, but many things happen that they can't quite understand. Plus, the house itself has a frightening quality about it. The story moves right along, with no possibility of the reader's losing interest. Just don't read it while home alone at night!

Okimoto, Jean Davies. **Who Did It, Jenny Lake?**   M

When a student wants to read a good mystery, I'm often caught short as to what to recommend. Therefore I was pleased to discover this novel, which is a mystery as well as a captivating story about a girl who is away at boarding school. Jenny Lake goes to Hawaii for spring vacation, and within a short time, a friend of her aunt is murdered right in the hotel where Jenny is staying. Jenny and her friend Freddie have some real adventures trying to discover who killed Harriet Van Pelte.

Paige, Harry W. **The Summer War.** E

This book tells a good mystery that I found both intriguing and terrifying. A camper, Ely Justin, discovers a corpse, long dead, in the woods near his camp. This discovery leads to an incredible adventure for Ely, one that he finds fascinating, as does the reader. The story reads very well and includes some very good characters of varied ages. I couldn't put it down.

Raskin, Ellen. **The Westing Game.** M

Raskin has succeeded in writing a book that tangled me up so much that I *had* to keep reading to clear up my confusion. She writes of Samuel W. Westing, a man who created a game in his will. If his heirs play this game well enough, they could become millionaires. And play they do—but the more they play, the more complicated the game gets. I loved reading this book, as do my students.

Roberts, Willo Davis. **The Pet-Sitting Peril.** M

Nick is an 11-year-old boy who takes care of people's pets as a summer job. Three of his clients live in the same building, an old Victorian which has been converted to apartments. A number of strange things happen in that building, and Nick is involved in a dangerous and thrilling way. This is another good story for lovers of mysteries.

White, Ellen Emerson. **Friends for Life.** M

This book I would classify as a thriller. Although it scared me, I did enjoy reading it; in fact, I found that I couldn't stop. When Colleen dies, her best friend Susan is sure she was murdered and sets out to prove it. In the process, Susan has to deal with a group of people at school who definitely live faster than she does, but she is convinced they were involved in whatever led to Colleen's death. It is clear that Susan herself is in danger as she investigates her friend's death; nonetheless, she is determined to find out just what happened.

Woolfolk, Dorothy. **Mother, Where Are You?** M

This mystery writer has developed a character who acts as an amateur detective: Donna Rockford. Donna is a college student who is eager to become a detective or a private investigator some day. She pursues this interest whenever something intriguing comes up. In this book, the intrigue surrounds a friend of hers who is adopted. When the girl's adoptive father dies, she wants to look for her real parents and enlists Donna's aid. This leads to some tough detective work for the two girls as well as some danger. The story is interesting and suspenseful, although the writing is weak.

Yep, Laurence. **Liar, Liar.** M

This contemporary novel tells the story of a boy named Sean who goes through an amazing experience when his friend Marsh dies in an automobile accident. Sean suspects that someone tampered with Marsh's car, and he sets out to prove it. However, he is not prepared for what he discovers—nor for the jeopardy in which this discovery puts his own life. During his investigations, Sean gets to know Marsh's sister, Nora. They become friends as they try to find out what caused Marsh's accident.

Yep, Laurence. **The Mark Twain Murders.**   M

During the Civil War, Mark Twain lived in San Francisco. He was a reporter, and not a very good one. Amazingly enough, he did solve a murder with the help of a 15-year-old boy who called himself the Duke of Baywater. Yep's fictional tale is based on actual events and offers a humorous introduction to Mark Twain. A reader might even look for stories by Mark Twain after reading this book!

Other books to consider:

Christie, Agatha. Many titles.

Duncan, Lois. **Killing Mr. Griffin, Summer of Fear, Daughters of Eve, They Never Came Home**, and others.

SUPERNATURAL, TIMEWARP, AND FANTASY BOOK LIST

Ames, Mildred. **Anna to the Infinite Powers.**   M

In the past few years we've heard friends make jokes about clones, referring to someone they'd like to have two of, or someone who is needed in two places at once. In this story, however, the matter of clones is no joke. Anna Zimmerman Hart is a clone, a fact she doesn't discover until she is 12 years old, and then only accidentally. She is the result of an experiment in which the government cloned a woman scientist, Anna Zimmerman, who had died. What they hoped to achieve was the possibility of completing the woman's scientific work through her clone. Young Anna is not exactly thrilled at discovering that she is not the normal girl she thought she was. In fact, her life becomes terribly frightening. I admit that I couldn't put this book down; I think almost anyone would enjoy reading it.

Barber, Antonia. **The Ghosts.**   M–H

When the Allen family moved to the caretaker's cottage of a large country house, the two children, Lucy and Jamie, never suspected the adventure that lay in store for them. They were to meet the ghosts of children who had lived in the house one hundred years earlier and who had died in a fire. Lucy and Jamie were able to help change the events of their lives, but they had to be very brave to accomplish that. This book was impossible to put down. It was great reading!

Bond, Nancy. **A String in the Harp.**   H

This book is similar to Susan Cooper's series that begins with *Over Sea Under Stone*. It is a fantasy adventure in which one character, Peter Morgan, is able to move backwards in time, though not actually leave his life in the 20th century. The Morgan children and their father are living in Wales for a year, their mother having died the previous year. The entire family has a hard time adjusting to her death as well as to their new locale. Peter is especially unhappy. Wandering alone one day, he finds an ancient harp-tuning key—the key that will take him back into other times. On these excursions he sees people who lived centuries earlier in this part of Wales. Generally, they don't see him or communicate in any way, but at times they do. Peter finds this situation disconcerting, but also very exciting. It's fascinating to read how these experiences change his view of life in Wales.

Cassedy, Sylvia. **Behind the Attic Wall.**   M

Maggie Turner is an orphan who has been to many different boarding schools. She just doesn't fit in anywhere. At every school she is the brunt of everyone's jokes and spends most of her time alone. Maggie eventually comes to live with two elderly aunts in a house that used to be a boarding school. In that house, she has the most amazing experience: she discovers in the attic two dolls who are "alive." She talks with them, has tea with them, and finds for the first time in ages that she is enjoying herself. Strange though it is, it does change Maggie's life for the better.

Johnston, Norma. **Timewarp Summer.**   M

My interest in the element of time drew me to this book. Although I enjoyed it, it is probably too old for junior high readers. The characters are in their last years of high school and experience things beyond the scope of junior high, or at least *my* junior high. However, the format is worth a look. The author quite cleverly lets the plot of the story determine her style. That is, she writes the book as a movie script, and in the story, her characters are themselves making a movie. That, in itself, is intriguing.

LeGuin, Ursula. **A Wizard of Earthsea.**   H

This is one of only a few books LeGuin has written specifically for children. Though it is very good, it should be considered fare for a good reader. The main character, Ged, is invited by a mage to study all aspects of magic with him. Ged is a very talented student, but he is also overly proud, too eager to use his powers when challenged. This pride lands him in a very precarious position. How he extricates himself from that dilemma is the focus of LeGuin's story. It is very intriguing fantasy.

Lunn, Janet. **The Root Cellar.** M

I always enjoy books in which the author manipulates time, and in this book, Lunn does it magnificently. Rose Larkin, an orphan since the age of three, has to go to live with her cousins' family after her grandmother dies. Rose immediately dislikes it at Aunt Nan's and one day hides in a root cellar to escape the family. When she emerges, she finds herself in the same place but *not* the same time. It is the 1860s, an era in which Rose immediately feels she belongs. Throughout the novel, Rose moves back and forth from the present to the past. She becomes involved in looking for a soldier who had fought in the Civil War. The story ends in a startling manner, but one that is very satisfying.

McKinley, Robin. **The Door in the Hedge.** H

This book includes four stories, two original and two that are retold. The reader who likes fairy tales will find these exceptional. The characters have problems that can sometimes be solved, but sometimes not. I was particularly intrigued by "The Twelve Dancing Princesses" as retold by McKinley. It is the traditional story: The king has offered a fine reward to the man who can discover the source of his daughters' strange behavior. They wear out a pair of dancing slippers each night, even though they are locked in their bedroom. A soldier, with some advice from an old woman, finally unravels the mystery. However, there is much more development of the man's character than I remember from the fairy tales I read as a child. That careful character development helps make these stories excellent ones. I found the book good reading, though not as good as *The Blue Sword* by the same author.

Park, Ruth. **Playing Beatie Bow.** H

Here is another author who allows her characters to go backward and forward in time in the most intriguing ways. Park sends Abigail Kirk back 100 years into the Australia of 1873— actually it was New South Wales at that time. Abigail becomes part of a family, much to her dismay, and remains in that earlier era for quite a while. She does finally return to 1973, but it is clear that she will never look at the city, its buildings, its people, its very atmosphere, in the same way again. The experience has a profound effect on her. This is a marvelous book for one who enjoys a good story.

Peck, Richard. **The Dreadful Future of Blossom Culp.**   M

Whenever I find an author I like, I always look for new books that person has written. I was delighted to find Peck's latest Blossom Culp book. Blossom has been a prominent character in two other good books, *The Ghost Belonged to Me* and *Ghosts I Have Been.* Here we find Blossom entering high school in Bluff City. The grade school principal has chatted with her about conforming more to the standards of the community—meaning that Blossom shouldn't use her "second sight" anymore, because it just gets her in trouble and makes her stick out as different. Anyway, that is Miss Spaulding's opinion. Of course, the fact remains that Blossom *is* different. Many interesting situations occur in her first two months of school, culminating in a very eventful Halloween. This book is delightful, fun, mysterious, and generally good reading.

Roberts, Willo Davis. **The Girl with the Silver Eyes.**   M

Katie is a normal-looking girl except for the color of her eyes: silver. Perhaps this quality is accentuated since she wears glasses. In any case, it certainly causes a negative reaction in other people. There's one other thing about Katie, too—she has the power to move things with her mind. Katie does not know why her eyes are a strange color, but when she discovers that there might be other young people with the same condition, she decides to look for them. Katie's search leads to some unusual adventures.

Rodowsky, Colby. **Keeping Time.**   M

Once again, here is an author who takes us back in time with the main character, Drew. He and his family are street musicians, or buskers. One day when they play "Greensleeves," Drew finds himself in London of another time, befriended by a musician's apprentice named Symon Ives. Drew makes several trips from his home in Baltimore back in time to the London of Queen Bess, always when the group plays "Greensleeves." This travel helps Drew learn to communicate better with his father, but it also makes him realize the importance of the style of entertaining he and his family do. The book reads very well.

Stolz, Mary. **Cat in the Mirror.**   M

Here we go again, back in time! Where do the past, present, and future exist? Like Madeleine L'Engle and Francine Pascal, Stolz explores this idea in her novel of Erin, a teenager who is having problems making friends, or of Irun, the Egyptian girl Erin becomes when she . . . well, is it a dream? Is it a concussion? Is it a journey? Whatever it is, Erin/Irun enjoys her stay in ancient Egypt and seems to gain some understanding from her adventure.

Voight, Cynthia. **Building Blocks.**   E

Here's yet another story that leads us back in time with the main character. Brann Connell takes a nap behind some building blocks that he has inherited from his father, who built with them as a child. When Brann wakes up, he doesn't know where he is and assumes he is dreaming. Soon he realizes that he is mistaken, but it still takes him a while to realize that he has gone back to the time when his father was a boy. In fact, he is in his father's childhood home. Brann learns a great deal about his father and the way he was raised, which helps him when he finally returns to his own time. This book is a good read.

Wiseman, David. **Blodwen and the Guardians.**   M

When I saw a new book by David Wiseman on the shelf, I was delighted. I loved *Jeremy Visick*, and I hoped this book would be equally good. I was not disappointed. The Lewis family has just moved to the country from the city. They have bought a house called Mow Cottage in a small village in England. Behind the cottage is a very mysterious grove. None of the villagers venture there, and many hold it in awe. The grove intrigues Blodwen, the 10-year-old Lewis girl, but she is kept away by the strange and frightening noises she hears whenever she walks in through her back gate. When workmen arrive to build a roadway through the grove, the villagers join with the "guardians" of the grove to convince everyone that it is best to leave the area untouched, in the state it has been for centuries. This is fantasy at its richest.

Wiseman, David. **Jeremy Visick.**   M

Here is another author who uses time as an important element of his story. Wiseman tells the story of 12-year-old Matthew Clemes. Matthew's history teacher responds to a challenge from the boy, who asserts that history is rubbish. To counter this claim, the teacher assigns Matthew to go to the cemetery near his house and write down the information on a particular tombstone. While Matthew is there, he finds a stone that interests him even more—one that records the death of a man and his two sons, plus a third son who also died but whose body lies in the mine shaft where their deaths occurred. This third son is Jeremy Visick. Matthew goes back to Jeremy's time and watches as Jeremy goes off to the mine with his father and two brothers. He and Jeremy are able to talk, but no one else is aware of Matthew's presence. Matthew eventually helps Jeremy, and the reader feels good about Matthew's commitment to his friend. This book has many good qualities; among them is the extensive, fascinating information on mining.

Wright, Betty Ren. **The Secret Window.**   E

Meg Korshak dreams, but she doesn't have ordinary dreams; she has dreams that are going to come true. Many times her dreams are frightening and not terribly clear. Other times, they feature people she knows and are very clear. This gift is sometimes a problem for Meg, but it eventually proves to be a wonderful quality. This is a good book about a girl and her relations with her family and friends. I couldn't put it down.

Other books to consider:

Chant, Joy. **Red Moon and Black Mountain: The End of the House of Kendreth.**

Harrison, Harry. **The Men from P.I.G. and R.O.B.O.T.**

Pinkwater, D. M. **Alan Mendelsohn, the Boy from Mars; The Hoboken Chicken Emergency; The Worms of Kukumlima.**

Tolkien, J.R.R. **The Silmarillion, The Hobbit, The Lord of the Rings** (a trilogy).

GENERAL FICTION BOOK LIST

Angell, Judi. **What's Best for You.**　E

Lee can't believe that her mother is really going to move to New York City, leaving Lee to stay with her father on Long Island. She tries to run away from her mother's apartment in New York City several times and succeeds in making her parents very worried. Lee finally understands that her parents just can't get along and that she will have to adjust to their divorce. This is a good book about a family situation.

Bethancourt, T. Ernesto. **T.H.U.M.B.B.**　E

This is an author whose books I invariably like, so I always start to read a new one with great eagerness. With this title I was not disappointed, but I was treated to a story very different from what I generally expect from Bethancourt. The two boys who star in this book are aspiring musicians who cook up wonderfully incredible schemes. They live and go to high school in Brooklyn. Though they want to perform in a rock group, they join the orchestra because it is the only performing group in school—then remake it into a wonderful band they call THUMBB, The Hippest Underground Marching Band in Brooklyn. What happens to them in this group makes terrific reading, and very funny, too.

Bond, Nancy. **The Best of Enemies.**　H

This book ought to be part of a fiction list for every eighth-grade social studies teacher. It is set in Concord, Massachusetts, where a Patriot's Day celebration is going to take place. A group of British men has arrived in Concord for the celebration, led by a Captain James MacPherson. For many years, the captain has corresponded with his old friend, Commodore Shattuck, carrying on a running argument about the strategy used in the Revolutionary War. Gradually it becomes clear that this year Captain MacPherson plans to refight one such battle, attacking the Minutemen at Old North Bridge while they are on parade. We follow these developments along with young Charlotte Paige who has involved herself in the planning of the celebration. The reading is great, both interesting and fun.

Bond, Nancy. **Country of Broken Stone.**   H

I loved Bond's *A String in the Harp*, but this story is not quite so compelling. I still loved it, though. Penelope, 14 years old, goes off to the North of England where her stepmother is to supervise an archaeological dig. Penelope finds little to do besides read, draw, and play with her eight-year-old stepsister. With time on her hands, Penelope goes off exploring and meets and makes friends with a local boy. Although this all sounds rather tame, it is very interesting to see how a 14-year-old girl from London relates to a boy of the same age from a remote farming area. They like each other, but they certainly operate differently and look at life from almost opposite vantage points. Bond writes for eager, rather mature readers.

Brancato, Robin F. **Sweet Bells Jangled out of Tune.**   M

Ellen Dohrmann is in an unusual situation. She lives with her mother in the same town where her grandmother lives a very eccentric life. In fact, Ellen's mother no longer sees her mother-in-law and has also forbidden her daughter to visit her. Ellen decides to disobey her mother because she so wants to talk to her grandmother. When she does, she discovers that all the utilities in her grandmother's large home have been turned off. The house is overflowing with odd items her grandmother is hoarding, and the weeds are waist high outside. Ellen also realizes that her grandmother is no longer responsible for herself; she knows that the old woman needs help. Although this upsets the girl very much, she does a fine job of getting the needed help for her grandmother. This is a touching story about a girl's sense of responsibility toward another person she loves.

Brancato, Robin F. **Winning.**   M

Since sports are such an important part of many young people's lives, I was eager to see how Brancato would deal with the life of a boy who is badly injured in a football game. Happily, she does a fine job. We meet Gary Madden in the hospital, unable to move as a result of his injury. He is miserable; his parents are miserable. His girlfriend is not sure how to act, nor are most of his friends. Brancato develops her characters in a most believable way. Nothing seems contrived.

Butterworth, W. E. **A Member of the Family.** M

The Lockwood family has a series of unusual experiences with dogs—twin Llewellin setters, a neurotic Doberman, even an Old English sheepdog. Tom Lockwood, the teenage boy in the family and a dog lover, plays a central role in this book, which includes funny, baffling, and sad incidents.

Byars, Betsy. **The Glory Girl.** M

This is a very unusual story, from my point of view. Anna Glory and her family are gospel singers who make their living traveling places to sing, mainly in churches but also in halls, gyms, and the like. They also sell recordings of their songs. Anna is the only one who can't sing. This bothers her until an understanding relative appears on the scene. He is her father's brother, Uncle Newt, a man who has been serving a prison sentence. Newt helps Anna see that she, too, is special.

Cameron, Eleanor. **Julia and the Hand of God** and **A Room Made of Windows.** M–H

These two books follow Julia Redfern's life as she grows from a young girl to a fairly sophisticated teenager who knows that she wants to be a writer. Julia's Uncle Hugh gives her a nicely bound book filled with blank pages on which she can write anything she wishes. She calls it her Book of Strangenesses, and it is the beginning of Julia's writing career. I liked these books that are set in Berkeley, California, where the author herself grew up. Julia is a fascinating character.

Clapp, Patricia. **I'm Deborah Sampson.** M

Deborah Sampson is a girl of the 1700s. Her mother is too poor to raise her, so she is sent to live with her cousin, an elderly woman who dies soon thereafter. She then goes to live with Mistress Thatcher, one of her cousin's friends, who also dies. Deborah's friend, Reverend Conant, places her with the Thomases, a family with eight sons. Deborah becomes very good friends with the boys and learns to do all they can do, including shooting a rifle. When the Revolutionary War breaks out, the older boys go off to war. Soon Deborah follows them, disguising herself as a man in order to fight. This situation is very revealing about the circumstances surrounding the war for independence. The books reads very well.

Cohen, Barbara. **Benny.**   E

Since I am the oldest of four children, I find reading about
children in other positions in their families quite educational.
Benny, 11, is the youngest of three and is babied in different
ways by varying members of his family. It's the 1930s, and
Benny has to help in his father's store after school. Benny's
only real love is baseball. He is a fine hitter, but unfortunately,
the games are after school when he is expected to work. His
father thinks sports are nice but unimportant. Benny's brother
shares that view, believing only academics are important. Benny's mother and sister want him to be happy, but they don't
have any real solutions. The story is very readable, as Cohen's
books generally are. I enjoyed it.

Cohen, Barbara. **Bitter Herbs and Honey.**   M

Cohen often writes about the problems of Jews who find themselves in a world that is predominantly Christian. Such is the
case in this story about Rebecca Levitsky, a high school senior,
who becomes interested in a boy in her class who is not Jewish.
She knows her mother will not approve of Peter van Ruysdaal,
so she refuses to let him come to her home, either to visit her
or to pick her up for a date. Rebecca agonizes over her decision
to see Peter anyway, but she likes him and thinks it is her right
to spend time with him. Cohen has woven Jewish holidays and
traditions into a story that she tells straightforwardly and sen-
sitively. The reader understands Rebecca's dilemma and respects
her for the choice she makes.

Cohen, Barbara. **Fat Jack.**   M

In Judy Goldstein's high school, the senior class play is a big
deal. During Judy's senior year, the woman who generally directs
the play, and does it well, isn't available. As a result, the class
has to find a new director. Finally a rather unapproachable
man, the school librarian, agrees to direct the play, but only if
the organizing committee agrees to certain stipulations. This
agreement results in an unlikely group being cast in the play,
Henry IV Part One, which in turn leads to many unexpected
relationships and circumstances. Cohen has written a book that
I found very difficult to put down—I loved it.

Cohen, Barbara. **The Innkeeper's Daughter** and **R, My Name is
Rosie.**   M

I am listing these two books together because they have the
same characters and settings. The three Gold children, Dan,

Rachel, and Rosie, live at the Waterbridge Inn which their mother owns and runs. The first book gives us a look at 16-year-old Rachel's life while the second book is written from 10-year-old Rosie's point of view. It is interesting that Cohen, the author, actually grew up in an inn which her mother ran after she was widowed, a fact that enhances the story's credibility. Both books are fast reading with many enjoyable details and events.

Cohen, Barbara. **King of the Seventh Grade.**   M

Many children have to attend classes for religious instruction after school; Vic Abrams is one. He is a seventh-grader who must attend Hebrew School twice a week to prepare for his Bar Mitzvah at age thirteen. The Hebrew teacher is terribly boring, and Vic amuses himself by making jokes at the teacher's expense. This makes the other students laugh and ultimately leads to Vic's being kicked out of class. What follows is a very thoughtful reaction on Vic's part and an examination of values. The story is a good one—funny, touching, and relatively true to life.

Cohen, Barbara. **Lovers' Games.**   M

This book of Cohen's is written for a slightly older audience than usual. I imagine eighth-grade girls would like it since it deals with a developing interest in boys; however, it is almost too advanced for junior high and too young for high school, if that is possible. Nonetheless, I enjoyed the story of two cousins getting all mixed up about which one likes which boy. It is funny to see how hard each one works to convince the other about whom she really likes. Of course, everything is straightened out in the end, and that is nice too.

Cohen, Barbara. **Thank You, Jackie Robinson.**   E

Twelve-year-old Sam Greene lives in an inn with his mother and three sisters. He is a baseball lover and a zealous Dodgers fan. When Davy comes to cook at the inn, Sam finds a true friend. Davy is a 60-year-old black man who follows the Dodgers as loyally as Sam does. The two become a real team in going to games, sharing information, and talking about their favorite subject, the Brooklyn Dodgers. When Davy has a heart attack, Sam gets him the only present he knows will mean anything: a baseball signed by the Dodgers, including his special hero Jackie Robinson. The friendship between Sam and

Davy is a wonderful one, and even the reader with no interest in baseball becomes caught up in what those two love most.

Colman, Hila. **Accident.**   M

This is a sensitive story about two teenagers who live in the same town and go to school together, but one is rich, the other poor. When Adam DeWitt asks Jenny Melino out, she is delighted. They go out on his motorcycle, but Jenny is accidentally thrown off and paralyzed. Adam is not hurt. Colman does a good job of showing the contrasting emotions of these two young people. While one is dealing with traumatic injuries, the other is dealing with traumatic feelings.

Colman, Hila. **The Family Trap.**   M

Because of the subject matter, this book is appropriate for an older reader than those in seventh or eighth grade, though in reading level it is certainly understandable by that age group. The author deals with the idea of a 16-year-old becoming legally responsible for herself. Becky Jones, 15, wants to become an emancipated minor because her father is dead, her mother is in an institution, and her older sister isn't an appropriate guardian for her—or so she thinks. Becky pursues this legal option amidst the turmoil of life with her older sister, Nancy, and her younger sister, Stacey. Although it was interesting for me to see their problems and how they resolve them, I couldn't imagine my students relating to these older characters. Perhaps in a few years they would enjoy this book more.

Conford, Ellen. **Lenny Kandell, Smart Aleck.**   E

The main character in this story is on his way to a career as a stand-up comic. Lenny Kandell is funny. At least, he makes his *friends* laugh, but his family finds him less than funny. His mother thinks he is irresponsible; his sister thinks he ought to grow up; his teacher thinks he daydreams too much. Actually, they are probably all right, but Lenny cares only about being funny. Any reader will enjoy this book, laughing both with Lenny and at him. He gets into some amazing predicaments that usually get worse the more he struggles to get out of them. Reading should be enjoyable, and Conford makes it so with this book.

Corcoran, Barbara. **Don't Slam the Door When You Go.**   M

It is not uncommon for teenagers to feel uncomfortable or unwelcome at home, but I generally expect them to respond by "acting out." Instead, the three girls in Corcoran's novel leave their homes to go live together on their own in Montana. Only one girl, Lily, has her father's blessing. Judith's and Flower's parents don't even know where they are. I enjoyed finding out how the girls coped with the problems of everyday living at only 17 years of age. The do fairly well!

Corcoran, Barbara. **Make No Sound.** M

In this book I enjoyed getting to know Melody, seeing how she deals with the problems that are created by her mother, her wild older brother Brian, and the family's move to Hawaii. Melody adjusts amazingly well to her new home under rather difficult circumstances. She makes friends with many different people, from Mr. Poha, the minister, to Mrs. Kealola, a neighbor. She also gets to know a radio personality whose late-night talk show offers her a pleasant escape from her troubles.

Christopher, Matt. **Dirt Bike Runaway.** E

The best aspect of this book is the motocross racing. The author's description of the action is both informative and exciting. Peter Lewinski runs away from his foster home and takes up motocross racing in another town. He runs into a tough crowd but eventually meets a nice boy who helps him straighten things out. The book reads fast and well.

Doty, Jean Slaughter. **Dark Horse.** E

I have found that there is always some demand for horse stories. Many readers find that once they reach seventh grade, they've read all the horse stories available. This book is a good addition to such a list. The story is told from Abby's point of view. Abby loves horses, though she doesn't have one and has no reason to believe she will acquire one. That doesn't keep her from becoming an important helper at the stable near her home. There Abby gets acquainted with Sandpiper, Sandy for short, a horse who arrives at High Hickory Farms thin and uncared for. Abby discovers that he is a jumper, and this leads to adventure. With her many opportunities to ride at High Hickory Farms, Abby becomes a good rider as well as a fine stable hand. I enjoyed this book for its characters as well as the plot.

Foley, June. **It's No Crush, I'm in Love.** M

This book provides a good laugh as well as a satisfying story. Annie Cassidy and her friend Susanna Siegelbaum, both high school freshmen, share conversations and adventures that center around Annie's belief that she is in love with her English teacher, Mr. Angelucci. Of course, the "affair" turns out badly, but the events surrounding it are interesting and enlightening.

Foley, June. **Love By Any Other Name.**   M

Although I didn't like this book much when I started it, I was hooked after a while. I was at first dismayed by the way the main character falls all over a boy, one Bubba Umlauf, a star athlete at the high school. Billie's behavior was too much for me at first, but she develops into a better character as the story continues. In fact, Billie matures from a smart-aleck to a fairly serious person, much to the relief of her parents and teachers, perhaps even to Billie herself. The love and dating angle of the book tends to limit its audience to girls, putting it in a genre that I find objectionable, but so be it. I did find myself caught up in the story.

Gauch, Patricia Lee. **Night Talks.**   H

As a girl, I never went to camp. Although that doesn't bother me and never did, I do believe that a camp experience can be a good one, offering the kinds of friendships and experiences that a young person might expect to have in college. Gauch writes about a group of high school girls at camp who have an exceptional counselor, Nikki, a young woman who fiercely wants "things" to happen—"things" being character-building experiences that the campers will never forget. Nikki tackles quite a group this particular summer, and she and the girls definitely share some unforgettable experiences. I found the characters intriguing and the story an involving one.

Goldman, Katie. **In the Wings.**   M

Jessie, a freshman in high school, has decided to try out for the school play, *The Prime of Miss Jean Brodie*. She is very excited when she gets a part in the play, but she has many tough times ahead of her, related to problems with her parents and her best friend, Andrea. While Jessie does well in the play, the rest of her life is rather shaky. She discovers that not everything works out the way you want it to, but you have to make the best of it anyhow. This book reads very quickly.

Greenwald, Sheila. **Will the Real Gertrude Hollings Please Stand Up?**   E

This is a wonderful story about a girl who doesn't fit in, at least not the way other people wish she did. Gertrude needs a tutor just to get by in school, even though she goes to a special school that other people consider easy. Gertrude isn't happy with herself, and no amount of positive thinking from her mother seems to help. The event that finally does help Gertie is a business trip to Greece for her parents. They can't take Gertie along, so they leave her with her cousin Albert and his parents. This proves to be quite an occasion for everyone, mostly hilarious for the reader. Gertie is a great kid whom anyone would enjoy getting to know.

Haas, Jessie. **Working Trot.** M

Now that I have been looking for books about horses for some of the girls in my class, I keep discovering new ones. This one is very good, though it would appeal to a slightly older reader. It is the story of an 18-year-old boy who decides *not* to go to college but to live instead on a horse ranch and perfect his ability at dressage. This is a major decision for him, but the education he gets on this ranch makes it well worthwhile. He finds the work incredibly hard but very rewarding. The story reveals a variety of characters, most of them hard-working, dedicated horse lovers, who approach life quite differently from average folk. It is good reading.

Hentoff, Nat. **This School Is Driving Me Crazy.** M

I laughed a lot as I read this book. Sam Davidson, a sixth grader in a private school in New York City, is such a funny boy. He does the most maddening things, both at home and at school. Eventually, he proves that he is not just crazy, he is honest and trustworthy, which makes his father feel much better.

Hermes, Patricia. **You Shouldn't Have to Say Good-bye.** M

I don't think I've read any other young adult fiction that deals so well with death. The Morrow family, 13-year-old Sarah and her parents, have to face and accept the fact that Mrs. Morrow is dying of cancer. They are terribly sad, as any family would be, but their behavior is very believable, which is most welcome in a novel of this sort. Mrs. Morrow is concerned about teaching Sarah the things she doesn't know how to do, as well as talking to her about subjects she feels are important. Sarah is reluctant to discuss death, for she wants to ward it off. Mr. Morrow tries to support both his wife and his daughter, a very heavy load for him. The reader is moved to tears on a number of occasions, but we feel positively about Sarah and her father and their ability to cope after Mrs. Morrow's death. This is a very good story!

Kay, Mara. One Small Clue.   M

This book offers vicarious experiences for the armchair traveler. The reader goes to Odessa, Russia, with Madge and John, two teenagers in search of their father. Their mother left him in Russia when she was 8 months pregnant, stowing away on a freighter going to the United States. She died when the children were born. Now, as teenagers, they discover that their father could still be alive in Russia, and they plan a trip there to try to locate him. The situation in Odessa is certainly different from that in the United States, and the reader is made very aware of the differences. The story held my attention throughout.

Kennedy, S. A. Hey, Didi Darling.   M

This book is such a good laugh! Five girls have a rock group, and though they are good, they find they can't get any jobs simply because they are girls. To solve the problem, their leader, Tammy, convinces them to dress as boys. They are doubtful at first, but the switch does help and the group is hired to play at a dance. Success is just around the corner. However, the girls do have problems appearing as boys. Those problems are hilarious for the reader.

Kennemore, Tim. Wall of Words.   M

In this book we are introduced to a family of four very different children. Early on, we learn that their father has been gone for about a year and a half, writing the great novel, leaving the mother to support the four girls alone. We get to know Kim the best, she is the oldest; but we also become well acquainted with eight-year-old Kerry, who seems to be suffering from school phobia. Anna, the youngest, wants to be a radio and TV personality. Frances, the 11-year-old, is the child on whom her mother depends. All four girls are distinct characters, and they come through some difficult times very well.

Kerr, M. E. Little Little.   M

This author kept me thoroughly entertained with her satirical approach to the subject of dwarfs. Although this may not sound like a very funny subject, Kerr certainly does a wonderful job of showing the reader that all of life's conditions have their funny side. Belle LaBelle is a dwarf, the daughter of very rich parents. They lavish on her all the attention they would if she were a normal size. However, they do it by insisting that she be the queen of the diminutives. The dwarfs have an organization called TADpoles, The American Diminutives. The antics of these people provide a good laugh, especially for a reader with a sophisticated sense of humor.

Klass, Sheila Solomon. **Alive and Starting Over.**   M

Jessica VanNorden does some real growing up in this novel as she copes with changes in life. She has a new stepmother. A new boy is interested in her, causing her to make certain decisions about her regular boyfriend. And, her grandmother's health seems to be fading. Faced with all of these circumstances, Jessica does some painful wondering about what life is all about. Her story reads well.

Knowles, Anne. **Under the Shadow.**   E

Although the front cover shows a boy being led on a horse, this is *not* a book about horses. It is a book about living with a handicap yourself, as well as relating to other handicapped people. When Cathy meets Mark, she is taken aback to learn that he has muscular dystrophy. He is a very direct person, almost too direct sometimes. Also, he is very grumpy when things aren't going well for him. If Cathy hadn't been both sensitive and attracted to Mark's sense of humor and interests, she might have avoided him. Instead, she becomes his good friend. She even convinces her father to buy a pony for Mark to ride, giving him the feeling of freedom he misses in his wheelchair. I really liked this book. The characters are nicely developed and the story moves well.

Levy, Elizabeth. **The Computer That Said Steal Me.**   M

Stealing is an issue that arises with children of many ages. It can be a real problem in the middle grades, especially if it is admired by the child's peer group. In this novel, Adam, a sixth grader, decides to steal a computer chess set. The story is told from Adam's point of view, so the reader learns firsthand what it feels like to steal. Adam is not generally the stealing type, but he does steal the computer, an expensive item. Not only does he regret it, he also feels great qualms about what to do about it. Although he finally solves his problem, it isn't easy, and the reader feels the agony that Adam suffers. I liked this book for its true-to-life characters in a realistic situation.

Mazer, Norma Fox. **Taking Terri Mueller.**   M

Terri Mueller is thirteen, living very happily with her father. According to her father, Terri's mother died when the girl was four; however, when Terri's aunt visits, Terri overhears a conversation between them that leads her to believe that they have been keeping information from her. She asks her father about her mother, but, as always, he refuses to talk about her. In response, Terri refuses to speak to him, until he finally supplies the aunt's address so that Terri can write to her. This leads to discoveries that change Terri's life. Mazer does a fine job of showing how characters react under difficult and emotionally charged circumstances.

McHargue, Georgess. **The Horseman's Word.**   H

Leigh goes to stay with her aunt and uncle in Scotland, to help out on their farm while Uncle Will recovers from a stroke. Her job is to take care of the ponies that carry sight-seeing tourists. During her stay in Scotland, Leigh meets a boy who proves to be an unusual new friend. Together, they discover some of the difficulties in life, but they also learn about keeping their word and being loyal to another person. This is a very good but difficult book to read. It is not for easily discouraged readers.

Paterson, Katherine. **Bridge to Terabithia.**   M

Girls are good athletes. I know that, but books generally seem to either overdo or downplay this idea. Paterson has struck dead center with the character Leslie Burke, a fifth grade girl who can run. She beats everyone, boys and girls alike. This leads to her friendship with Jess Aarons, who had planned to be the best runner in the fifth grade until Leslie moved in. I could read and believe. What a pleasure!

Paterson, Katherine. **Rebels of the Heavenly Kingdom.**   H

I do enjoy Paterson's books, but she has a writing style that can be challenging, and that is the case in this book. It is the story of a boy, Wang Lee, who is kidnapped from his home in China in the 1850s and becomes part of a group of rebels fighting to defeat the Manchu emperor. For me, the best part of the story involves a group of women warriors on horseback who use bows and arrows. They are a valiant and mysterious group, credited with many daring moves. Paterson gives the reader a good sense of Chinese history over a period of three years.

Sachs, Marilyn. **The Fat Girl.** M

This book is quite different from what I usually expect when I pick up an adolescent novel. Although the author does tell a story, she concentrates more on people's actions, reactions, and motivations, an emphasis more commonly found in adult fiction. For that reason, the book will not appeal to so wide a range of readers as others by Sachs. Still, readers who find people fascinating and enjoy learning what makes them tick will enjoy this book. A high school boy, Jeff, who is very good looking and thinks a great deal of himself, finds a fat girl in his ceramics class disgusting. One day he says something nasty about her that she overhears. Upset that he has caused the girl such grief, Jeff takes steps to apologize and gets carried away. Fascination leads to passion and then betrayal. The entire process is very revealing—of Jeff, of Ellen (the fat girl), of Jeff's former girlfriend, and of several members of his family. I came away feeling quite taken aback by the way people use others in this story.

Sachs, Marilyn. **Fourteen.** E

Sachs spoke in this area, and I went to hear her. Now that I've actually met the woman, I seem to enjoy her books even more. She related clearly how her own life, her own family, and her own circumstances give her the material for the books that she writes. In *Fourteen*, she pokes fun at herself by including a character who is a mother and a writer and who uses her own family in her books. The story deals with two 14-year-olds who solve an interesting mystery. They also fall in love, sort of. The book is fast and good reading.

Sachs, Marilyn. **Call Me Ruth.** E

Rifka Zelitsky is eight years old when she and her mother finally sail to the United States to join her father who is already settled in New York City. Rifka changes her name to Ruth when she moves to America. Her experiences as a young Jewish girl, newly arrived from Russia, are mixed—some joyous, some painful. She loves America, embracing all those things she sees as American: Thanksgiving, speaking English, wearing certain clothes. Yet in her eagerness to conform, Ruth runs into conflict with her mother, who is struggling as an immigrant. The book is timely, for many new American families from other shores have similar situations. This is a good story about a family, about being new in a country, and about the differences between the generations.

Shyer, Marlene Fanta. **Adorable Sunday.**   E–M

Can you imagine being named Sunday? That is what Mr. and Mrs. Donaldson named their first child, and she wasn't even born on a Sunday. Actually, Sunday's life is quite normal until her mother decides she is adorable. This occurs when Mrs. Donaldson sees a picture of her daughter after her braces have been removed. After that, there is no stopping the woman: she decides that Sunday has a promising career as a TV model. All of this naturally changes Sunday's life, not always for the better. Shyer writes a telling portrayal of Sunday's family and friends as the girl becomes a "star."

Skurzynski, Gloria. **The Tempering.**   H

I am a strong advocate of novels that present historical periods in a realistic way while telling a good story about interesting people. That is what happens in this novel, which gives the reader a clear view of life in a mill town in the early 1900s. Karl is 15 years old and will leave school on his 16th birthday to work in a steel mill, like all the other working class boys in his town of Canaan, Pennsylvania. Although he knows the work is hard and dangerous, it is what he has always wanted to do. Karl begins to change his mind when he meets his English teacher in September. She is very eager to keep the boys in school, and she does a good job of convincing Karl, partly because he falls in love with her. Certain events cause everyone's plans to change, and the resulting story definitely keeps the reader's interest.

Snyder, Zilpha Keatley. **The Birds of Summer.**   H

This book left me feeling very sad about Summer McIntyre and her little sister Sparrow. Even though by the end of the story things are looking up for the girls in some ways, their lives have already been so tough, tougher than they should have been. We see the story from 16-year-old Summer's point of view. Their mother is spending time with a man that Summer can't stand; furthermore, she seems to be involved in something mysterious, probably illegal, that could land all of them in trouble. I was particularly impressed with this teenage girl who looks after her seven-year-old sister in an incredibly adult manner.

Stanek, Lou Willett. **Megan's Beat.**   M

I've always know how different junior high is from high school, but this very good book draws the reader's attention to that difference. Megan Morgan graduates from Heckathorne, a country elementary school. In the fall she enters Sagamon High School, where country kids are considered hicks. Megan is determined to prove everyone wrong. In the process, she makes new friends but creates some enemies out of old friends. Then she reverses herself and gets her old friends back but jeopardizes her *new* friendships. This is a confusing time for Megan. Even so, she manages to learn a lot about herself in the decisions that she ends up making.

Strasser, Todd. **Friends Till the End.**   M

A number of significant things happen to David Gilbert during his senior year in high school: his soccer team wins the state championship; his girlfriend breaks up with him and then wants to go steady again; and he meets a new boy named Howie Jamison. David doesn't really get to know Howie until he finds out that the new boy has leukemia and is in the hospital. When David visits Howie, he rather likes him, but the friendship intrudes on David's life, and life may never be the same for David once this year is over. Strasser does a fine job of showing how people react to someone who is seriously ill.

Tate, Eleanora E. **Just an Overnight Guest.**   E

Being the oldest child in my family, I can't quite imagine what it's like to be the baby. Nine-year-old Margie Carson enjoyed that position in her family and didn't want to give it up. When a four-year-old named Ethel Hardisen came to stay, supposedly only for the weekend, Margie was miserable and remained so for a long time. Gradually Ethel learned to be nicer and better-behaved than she was when she first arrived, but Margie resented her even then. The story unfolds from Margie's point of view, which helps the reader understand her problems better.

White, Ellen Emerson. **The President's Daughter.**   M–H

Meg is a junior in high school, and, of all things, her mother is running for president. Furthermore, she actually wins the nomination *and* the election. Although this does change Meg's life somewhat, her mother has always been in politics and never home very much. Because of her infrequent contact with her mother, Meg finds it difficult to communicate with her when she is around. The book develops this theme well in a very involving story.

Yep, Laurence. **Child of the Owl.**   M

Yep is an author every teacher should read. A Chinese-American, he has written several books illustrating the Chinese experience in America. In this one, he introduces Casey Young, a Chinese girl who, after growing up in central California, has to go to live with her grandmother in San Francisco's Chinatown. Up to this time, Casey had never really thought about herself as Chinese, but once she arrives in Chinatown, she begins to see many things differently. She learns a great deal from her grandmother, as well as from other people she meets there. We see Casey emerge as a Chinese-American girl, proud of her Chinese heritage as well as her native land, America.

Yep, Laurence. **Dragonwings.**   H

When eight-year-old Moon Shadow travels from China to join his father, Windrider, in San Francisco, he is frightened. Ahead of him are many experiences, all new and different. He sees "demons" for the first time. He lives through an earthquake. He helps build the glider that his father has long dreamed of flying. Moon Shadow discovers that some demons are fine people and even makes good friends with two of them, Miss Whitlaw and her niece, Robin. This is another excellent Yep novel.

Yep, Laurence. **The Serpent's Children.**   M

One of the values of reading about people of other cultures is the insight we get into the lives they lead. In this book by Yep, we go back into the past to see what happens to the Young family as they live through the years of revolution in China. The mother dies, the father is injured while fighting, and the daughter, Cassia, becomes the real pillar of the family. The boy, Foxfire, eventually sails to America, the Golden Mountain. The Chinese point of view from which the story is written is fascinating as well as informative. Yep tells a good story, but its value goes way beyond that.